Buddhism

Religions of the World

Series Editor: Ninian Smart

Buddhism

Bradley K. Hawkins

California State University, Long Beach

Prentice Hall Inc., Upper Saddle River, NJ 07458

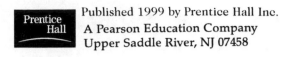
Published 1999 by Prentice Hall Inc.
A Pearson Education Company
Upper Saddle River, NJ 07458

Copyright © 1999 Calmann & King Ltd

ISBN 0-13-576604-4

This book was designed and produced by Calmann & King Ltd, London

Editorial work by Melanie White and Damian Thompson
Pronunciation guide by Heather Gross
Design by Design Deluxe and Karen Stafford
Map by Andrea Fairbrass
Artworks by Sarah-Jayne Stafford
Picture research by Peter Kent
Printed in China

Reviewers Theodore M. Ludwig, Valparaiso University; Tadanori Yamashita, Mount Holyoke University; Martha Ann Selby, Southern Methodist University

Picture Credits

Cover Jean-Léo Dugast, Panos Pictures; *page 18* Jean-Léo Dugast, Panos Pictures; *22* Takamasa Inamura, Sakamoto Photo Research Laboratory; *26* Sarah Errington, Hutchison Library; *31* Museum Rietberg, Zurich, Von der Heydt Collection/Foto Wettstein and Kauf; *41* Government Museum, Mathura; *51* Werner Forman Archive/Philip Goldman Collection; *66* Rex Features/Sipa/J. Torregnano; *74* Spectrum Colour Library; *96* Carlos Reyes-Manzo, Andes Press Agency; *107* Ted Streshinsky/Corbis

Contents

Foreword

Religions of the World

The informed citizen or student needs a good overall knowledge of our small but complicated world. Fifty years ago you might have neglected religions. Now, however, we are shrewder and can see that religions and ideologies not only form civilizations but directly influence international events. These brief books provide succinct, balanced, and informative guides to the major faiths and one volume also introduces the changing religious scene as we enter the new millennium.

Today we want not only to be informed, but to be stimulated by the life and beliefs of the diverse and often complicated religions of today's world. These insightful and accessible introductions allow you to explore the riches of each tradition—to understand its history, its beliefs and practices, and also to grasp its influence upon the modern world. The books have been written by a team of excellent and, on the whole, younger scholars who represent a new generation of writers in the field of religious studies. While aware of the political and historical influences of religion these authors aim to present the religion's spiritual side in a fresh and interesting way. So whether you are interested simply in descriptive knowledge of a faith, or in exploring its spiritual message, you will find these introductions invaluable.

The emphasis in these books is on the modern period, because every religious tradition has transformed itself in the face of the traumatic experiences of the last two hundred years or more. Colonialism, industrialization, nationalism, revivals of religion, new religions, world wars, revolutions, social transformations have not left faith unaffected and have drawn on religious and anti-religious forces to reshape our world. Modern technology in the last 25 years—from the Boeing 747 to the world wide web—has made our globe seem a much smaller place. Even the moon's magic has been captured by technology.

We meet in these books people of the modern period as a sample of the many changes over the last few centuries. At the same time, each book provides a valuable insight into the different dimensions of the religion: its teachings, narratives, organizations, rituals, and experiences. In touching on these features, each volume gives a rounded view of the tradition enabling you to understand what it means to belong to a particular faith. As the Native American proverb has it: "Never judge a person without walking a mile in his moccasins."

To assist you further in your exploration, several useful reference aids are included. Each book contains a chronology, map, glossary, pronunciation guide, list of festivals, annotated reading list, and index. A selection of images provide examples of religious art, symbols, and contemporary practices. Focus boxes explore in more detail the relation between the faith and some aspect of the arts—whether painting, sculpture, architecture, literature, dance, or music.

I hope you will find these introductions enjoyable and illuminating. Brevity is supposed to be the soul of wit: it can also turn out to be what we need in the first instance in introducing cultural and spiritual themes.

Ninian Smart
Santa Barbara, 1998

Preface

This is perhaps the appropriate place to comment on what the reader holds in his or her hand. It is a key, a key to the treasures of one of the oldest and most fascinating religions of humanity. As such, it is aimed at providing the first-time reader with a brief overview of the philosophy, history, and (most importantly) the "feel" of Buddhism. But it is only the first of many keys to a vast treasury. Since, as the reader is about to find out, Buddhism has changed and developed considerably over the 2,500 years of its existence, the treatment of each individual topic must necessarily be brief. Fortunately, the reader who wishes to delve more deeply into the ocean of Buddhism will find no lack of more detailed studies on almost any conceivable topic of interest. The Buddhists have a saying to the effect that after people have had the moon pointed out to them, the help of a pointing finger is no longer required. It is the author's hope that this small offering will be like that pointing finger, useful at the start of the reader's journey of discovery of one of the noblest products of the human spirit.

Bradley K. Hawkins
March 1998

Chronology of Buddhism

B.C.E.	Event
560	The traditional date of the birth of the Buddha.
531	The Buddha renounces his life as a prince and becomes an ascetic.
525	The Buddha achieves Enlightenment and begins to preach.
480	The traditional date of the Buddha's death.
c. 480	First Buddhist Council at Rajagriha in Bihar; the Vinaya and Sutra texts standardized.
386	Second Buddhist Council at Vaisali; first division of the Buddhist Order.
244	Third Buddhist Council called by Asoka; the canon of Theravadin Buddhism fixed.
c. 240	Buddhism introduced into Sri Lanka.
c. 100	Beginnings of Mahayana Buddhism.
c. 50	The Buddhist scriptures first written down in Sri Lanka.

C.E.	
c. 50	Central Asian merchants introduce Buddhism into northern China; first period of translation of Buddhist texts into Chinese begins.
c. 100	Fourth and last general Buddhist Council convened by Kaniska.
c. 200	Buddhism introduced to Southeast Asia by merchants.
c. 300	Buddhism begins to become a prominent religion in China; Buddhism begins to penetrate Korea.
402	The Chinese pilgrim Fa-hsian travels to India in search of Buddhist texts; initiates second period of translation of foreign Buddhist texts into Chinese.

B.C.E. indicates Before the Common Era.   C.E. indicates the Common Era.

538	Buddhism introduced into Japan from Korea.
630	The Chinese pilgrim Hsuan-tsang travels to India.
c. 750	Buddhism officially established in Tibet; beginnings of the Vajrayana school.
c. 750	Construction of Borobudur in Indonesia.
c. 800	Ch'an and Pure Land Buddhism become dominant schools in China; establishment of Tendai and Shingon schools in Japan.
c. 1050	Theravada Buddhism becomes official religion of Burma; other forms of Buddhism flourish throughout Southeast Asia.
1073	Foundation of the Sakyapa Monastery in Tibet; beginning of reform movement in Vajrayana Buddhism.
c 1175	Rinzai school of Zen established in Japan.
c. 1200	Muslim invaders deal the death blow to Buddhism in India after a long period of decline.
c. 1200	The Pure Land (Jodo) school of Buddhism is established in Japan.
c. 1240	The Soto school of Zen established in Japan.
c. 1250	The True Pure Land (Shin Jodo) school of Buddhism is founded in Japan.
c. 1300	Theravada Buddhism becomes official religion of Thailand; Cambodia soon follows.
c. 1360	Theravada Buddhism established in Laos.
c. 1350	Tsongkhapa founds the Gelugpa school of Vajrayana; this school comes to dominate Vajrayana Buddhism and is headed by the Dalai Lama.
c. 1870	Immigration from China and Japan begins to bring Buddhists into Hawaii and the western United States.
1880	Henry Steele Olcott begins campaign to revive Buddhism in Sri Lanka.
1881	Pali Text Society established to translate the Theravada scriptures into English.

1893	World Parliament of Religions in Chicago introduces Americans to Buddhism.
1931	Buddhist Society of America is founded in New York City for the study of Zen.
1931	Strongly nationalistic Buddhist society Nichiren Shoshu Soka Gakkai founded in Japan; still active.
1944	Buddhist Churches of America formed to unite the various North American Pure Land Buddhist groups.
1949	Communists come to power in China; beginnings of the repression of Buddhism.
1950	2500th year of Buddhism celebrated by large gathering in Burma.
c. 1950	First Zen groups become active in America.
1956	B. R. Ambedkar revives Buddhism in India.
c. 1965	Conflicts in Southeast Asia bring Buddhism to the attention of the American general public; first teachers of the Theravadin tradition come to America.
1967	Cultural Revolution in China; many treasures of Chinese Buddhism destroyed.
1968	First teachers of the Vajrayana school begin to teach in America.
1975	Khmer Rouge take power in Cambodia; many Buddhist monks murdered.
c. 1980	Nationalistic tendencies among some Buddhist monks in Sri Lanka contribute to the development of civil war in Sri Lanka.

Theravada: The Way of Discipline

The beautiful island of Sri Lanka lies off the southeast coast of India. Only a few degrees north of the equator, it is a lush green tropical land. It is also the oldest continuously Buddhist country on earth. The marks of Buddhism can be seen everywhere. In the ancient and now deserted capital cities of the north, Anuradhapura and Polonnaruwa, vast ruins attest to the devotion of former Sri Lankan kings to the Buddhist religion. In Polonnaruwa, huge statues of the Buddha were hewn out of the rock and these silent messengers from the past still command reverence today. But Buddhism is not just a dead relic of a glorious past. In present day Sri Lanka, some 75 percent of  the island's population still follows the precepts of the founder of Buddhism, Siddhartha Gautama, as Buddhists have done since the beginnings of the religion in c. 500 B.C.E. Moreover, many Sri Lankans elect to pursue their religion more deeply through entrance into the *Sangha*—the Buddhist Order of monks and nuns. Today, there are no official Buddhist nuns in Sri Lanka, but this was not always the case. Buddhism has long been noted for its positive attitude toward women, and women have pursued **Enlightenment** on an almost equal footing with men for much of its history.

For the Sri Lankans, Buddhism is a living faith that shapes their entire lives. Nowhere is this more evident than in Kandy, the capital of the last independent kingdom to exist in Sri Lanka before it began to be governed by the British in 1815. Built in a sheltered valley deep in the central hill country, Kandy has long been considered the center of Buddhism in Sri Lanka. The Kandyans' devotion to Buddhism is evident wherever one looks. By its central lake lie two of the most sacred Buddhist sites in Sri Lanka. On one side lies the Dalada Maligava, the Temple of the Tooth, so called because it houses a supposed relic of the Buddha—one of his teeth. Across the lake from the Dalada Maligava is Malvatta, the great central monastery of the Siyam Nikaya, the largest single group of Buddhist monks on the island. Not far away, at the other end of town is the other major monastery in Kandy. This is Asgiri, the central monastery of the second largest group of monks. Throughout the town and in the surrounding countryside, numerous tiny shrines and monastic residences attest to the popular devotion of the common people to their religious roots.

But not all Buddhist buildings in Sri Lanka are old. About five or six miles south of Kandy, in the mountains, there is a new Buddhist community. Built into the steep hillside, it serves as a center both for the local population and for interested foreigners who want to sample Buddhist culture. Like all **Theravada** Buddhist establishments, it presents the foreigner with two seemingly contradictory pictures of Buddhism. On the one hand, the shrines to the Buddha are sumptuous, colorful, and complex. On the other hand, the monks live in surroundings of utmost simplicity. Yet these contradictory images can be seen to form a seamless whole in the Theravadin worldview. Buddhists believe both that life is ultimately an unsatisfactory experience and that after we die we are reborn into the world time after time. This cycle of death and rebirth is called *samsara*. The many gorgeous shrines dedicated to the Buddha are constructed to honor the great teacher who revealed to human beings the way to escape from the pain of *samsara*.

Upon entering the monastery, one sees first the great stone arch that marks the boundary between the regular everyday secular world and the sacred world of the monastery. No elaborate

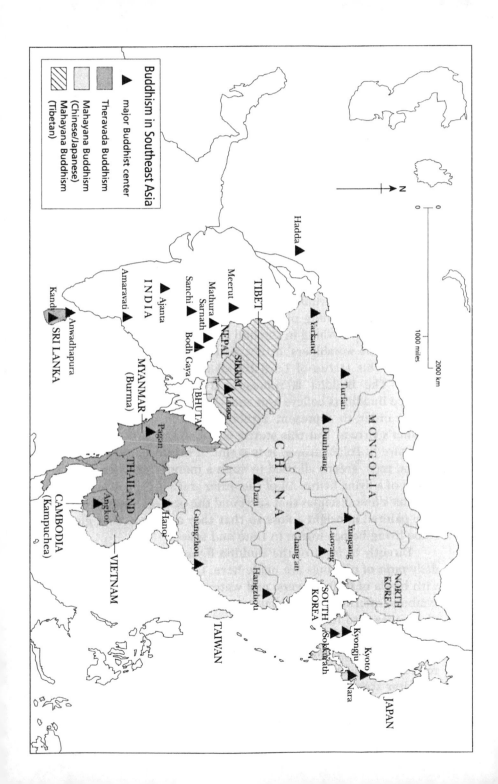

sign marks this division, just a stone gate surmounted by a carved wheel with eight spokes. In a sense, this simple emblem contains the entire teaching of the Buddha. The eight spokes symbolize the **Eightfold Path** which the Buddha advocated as the way to achieve release from the pains of the everyday world. The central hub of the wheel represents *Nirvana*, the goal toward which all Buddhists strive. *Nirvana* is something which is so different from the world that we experience that it cannot be described. But, in the truest sense, it is eternal peace.

Crowning the monastery at the top of the hill is the main shrine dedicated to the Buddha. On entering this shrine, one is cradled in cool semidarkness. The interior is lit only by the light from a few narrow windows placed high on the room's walls, and some candles burning on the altar. Instinctively, all conversation ceases. Everything in the hall is designed to quiet the mind and draw the worshipers' attention to the central figure of the Buddha. This statue of Lord Buddha stands some 15 feet in height. The Buddha is represented as being this tall, not because Buddhists believe him actually to have been this height, but in order to represent symbolically the greatness of the Buddha's virtues. But this statue is not the chaste, bare, stone sculpture of Polonnaruwa. It is a riot of bright colors, oranges, blacks, reds, greens all used in such a manner as to create the image of a living being. All of the other statues representing the Buddha's first disciples that surround the central figure are likewise painted in bright colors so that they appear at first glance to be living beings frozen in time and space.

Directly in front of the Buddha figure lies the altar. Since daily *puja* of offerings are made here, the altar table is covered with bowls of fruit, flowers, and water. This practice of making symbolic offerings rather than sacrificing animals (or even people) appears to have been originated by the Buddhists, and to have spread from them to Hinduism, the other great religion of India. Its intent is not to bribe or appease an angry deity, but to render thanks and praise to a revered teacher. On either side of the altar stand candlesticks for the candles that form the symbolic offerings of light. The faint sweet smoky scent of incense is everywhere. Around the walls are yet other figures which graphically depict the life and teaching of the Buddha. Most of the time, the only ones who attend the daily *puja* are the monks who live here. This changes on the days of the new moon and the full moon. These days, called in Sri Lanka **poya days**, are Theravadin holy days, and many villagers join the monks in their religious devotions.

Just below the shrine are the other monastery buildings. On the right, there is a large building which is used as a school. Here, regular classes are held for children in order to teach them the basics of the Buddhist religion. Here too, classes are held for interested foreigners. When not being used for religious teaching, the school rooms are used as a regular school. This link between Buddhism and education has been present since the very beginning of the religion. Other buildings house the guests' sleeping quarters, administrative offices, and the kitchen. This kitchen is something of an innovation.

Traditionally, Theravadin Buddhist monks, with their shaven heads and distinctive orange robes, have gone out at about nine o'clock in the morning and begged their food from house to house in nearby villages. The food was collected in large bowls that each monk carried by means of a cloth strap slung over his shoulder. After collecting their food, the monks would return to the monastery and eat before noon, since monastic rules forbid eating any solid food any later. Nowadays, with the influx of foreign students, the monks at this particular monastery decided to install a kitchen. They do not, however, do their own cooking. This is still forbidden. Rather, women from the village vie for the honor of cooking the monks' food. For Buddhist lay people, to give things to the monks or to perform service for them is a sure way to gain merit and a better rebirth.

Further down the slope, away from the hustle and bustle of the main compound, are the actual living quarters of the monks themselves. Each monk has his own hut. In his dwelling, the monk has a bed, a desk and chair, and perhaps some books. How the monk spends his day generally depends on his assigned duties. In Theravada countries, monks are generally divided

Theravadin monks in Thailand collect alms from passers-by. By supporting monks, laypeople acquire merit for this lifetime and subsequent ones.

informally into two groups. The first of these are the village monks whose main job is teaching and serving the needs of lay Buddhists. The forest monks form the second, much smaller group. Their main activity is meditating. Until recently, centers that specialized in teaching meditation to lay people did not exist. The major activity of lay persons was the gaining of merit through providing the monks with the necessities of life such as food, clothing, and medicine. Meditation was an activity practiced only by the monks. Now in Theravada countries there is a movement toward lay meditation as well, and centers have sprung up to teach meditation techniques to lay people.

While the Kandyan center is not strictly designed as a hermitage for forest monks, a number of its inhabitants follow that way of life. This means that they withdraw as much as possible from contact with the world. Thus the monk who wishes to follow this particular path must change his life radically. He ceases to interact with his family and friends. He ceases to meet with the general public except at a few ritual events throughout the year. These restrictions have a clear goal—to reach *Nirvana*. In order to accomplish this goal, the monks believe that they must live disciplined lives. That discipline comes from the rules of conduct established some 2500 years ago by the Buddha and later written down in the first of the three collections of scripture in Buddhism—the **Vinaya**.

This discipline is the essential foundation of the monks' religious practice. It is only after gaining control of their bodies and minds through this life of discipline that the monks can begin to meditate effectively. However, learning to meditate is not easy. The monks must spend many hours in perfecting their meditative technique. An extensive literature has sprung up describing this technique. This literature discusses the eight progressive stages of knowledge (*jnana*), the achievement of mental peace (*samatha*), and finally the deep, insightful meditation (*vipasyana*) that leads to Enlightenment and the end of rebirth.

Zen: The Way of Meditation

Given this ever present emphasis on meditation, it is not surprising that the monks in other parts of the Buddhist world developed meditative techniques appropriate to their own societies. One of the most radical of these schools is the form of Buddhism known in the West by the generic term **Zen**. In some ways, a Zen Buddhist monastery has a feeling to it that is remarkably similar to that of a Theravada Buddhist monastery. There is the same sense of quiet and of serious purpose. But in many other ways, there is a real difference as well. Even the monks look different. Like their Theravadin cousins, they shave their heads, but instead of loose orange robes, these monks wear somber black ones more fitted to the colder climates of northeast Asia.

A good example of both the similarities and the differences between Sri Lankan and Japanese monks can be seen at the **Soto** Zen head monastery of Eihei-ji. This monastery was founded in 1243 by the great Japanese Zen master Dogen. Built in the isolated and heavily forested mountains of western Japan, this monastery is still noted for the rigor of its training discipline. One can see the emphasis that Zen places on interior introspection in the very architecture of the monastery. Eihei-ji is surrounded by a blank wall with only one or two gates that are typically left closed and barred. But once one goes inside, a whole new world opens up.

Like most traditional Japanese monasteries, Eihei-ji is constructed around a series of courtyards. These courtyards often contain small gardens, either planted with live plants or rendered symbolically by means of abstract arrangements of rocks and sand. The rooms are separated by screens of rice paper and the floors are covered with *tatami*, mats of woven rushes which give the rooms a distinctive smell. These rooms are often bare of furniture, being furnished only with a few cushions. At night, the rooms double as sleeping quarters when sleeping pads called *futons* are taken from nearby cupboards and unrolled. The only decoration may be a small wall niche in which hangs a simple ink painting, or perhaps a pithy Zen saying in fine ink-brushed calligraphy. In front of this sits a small vase with a few carefully arranged flowers.

This austere simplicity is designed to promote a calm and peaceful atmosphere conducive to meditation. Many of the monks training in the monastery will be there for only a relatively brief period of time. In Japan, it has become the custom to allow monks to marry. This is not the case in most schools of

Buddhism. It has also become the custom for sons to inherit their fathers' positions as heads of the local Zen temples scattered throughout Japan. In order to do so, however, they must prove that they have attained a certain degree of proficiency in meditation. This is acquired through a two or three year course of training in the monastic setting. Only a few monks choose to dedicate their entire life to the quest for Enlightenment and spend their entire lives in the monastery.

The training schedule in Eihei-ji is not for the weak. Whereas in Theravada countries monks tend to have their own separate living space, in Zen monasteries the monks often live in dormitories. Monks are awakened before sunrise and bathe in cold water. Then they proceed to the shrine room and conduct the morning worship service. It has been assumed by many Europeans and Americans that Zen is a faith without ritual or scriptures. This is because the earliest writers on Zen in European languages emphasized meditation, often to the point that they ignored or downplayed other aspects of Zen practice. In fact, as is the case in other schools of Buddhism, Zen has many colorful and complex rituals designed to pay homage to the Buddha.

But for the true Zen practitioner, all of these actions are used to deepen their meditation. When a Zen monk goes to the bathroom, sits down to eat, or gets ready for bed, there is a prescribed ritual. Indeed, the entire life of the Zen monk is defined by such rituals. It must be remembered that these rituals are not seen as being important in themselves. Rather they are viewed as a means to an end. Their goal, like that of the code of discipline of the Theravadin monks, is to sharpen the monk's attention so that he is consciously aware of everything that he does. This "paying attention" is called **mindfulness** and has always been seen in Buddhism as one of the primary ways of achieving Enlightenment.

After morning worship, the monks of Eihei-ji begin the first of several periods of meditation that last between an hour and an hour and a half. The first thing that Zen meditators are taught is the proper posture for meditation. This is to sit cross-

legged on the floor in what is known as the **lotus position**. The buttocks are elevated by means of a cushion so that the back is straight and the head erect. The hands are folded in the lap.

There are two basic forms of Zen meditation. The first, practiced by the Soto school, consists of emptying the mind and achieving a deep meditative state. This is accomplished through techniques such as paying attention to one's breathing. If one penetrates deeply enough into this meditative state, hold the Soto practitioners, one will come to the realization of the true nature of reality and thereby achieve Enlightenment. The second method, practiced by the **Rinzai** school, has the same goal. It differs from Soto in its use of *koans*. A *koan* is a form of riddle that seems to have no logical answer. The point of the exercise is to use the *koan* to break through dualistic mundane logic and thus come to know the true nature of reality.

After meditation, the monks can at last have something to eat. The diet at a Zen monastery tends to be vegetarian. Unlike Theravada monks, who are allowed to eat meat if it has not been killed specifically for them, Zen monks must take no animal protein. This is why so much emphasis is placed on eating vegetable proteins such as are found in bean curd and on the proper balance of different food types. This has been popularized in Europe and America as the macrobiotic diet. Nor are the monks allowed to smoke or drink, at least while they are in training. Like all of their other activities, eating and cleaning up afterward is done in a deliberate, ritualistic way. After breakfast, they undergo more meditation practice until the middle of the afternoon, when another meal is taken. Then they disperse to attend to the maintenance of the monastery and their own few belongings. The day ends near sunset with another worship service. After this, the monks are allowed either to sleep or, if they wish, to meditate on their own into the night.

Zen monks follow prescribed rituals in order to achieve "mindfulness," the state of "paying attention" that deepens meditation and helps to achieve the goal of Enlightenment.

Vajrayana: The Way of Ritual

All of the Buddhist schools see meditation as being central to their religious practice. But each school has its own defining ritual characteristics. This was evident not very long ago in New York City. Imagine, if you will, Madison Square Gardens filled to overflowing. Not an unusual sight, since the Gardens are often packed with fight fans or people cheering on their favorite ice hockey team. But on the floor of the Gardens is not a sports team, but rather one man seated on a raised platform dressed in brightly colored robes. Around him are others dressed only slightly less elegantly and wearing tall feathered yellow hats. These people are chanting in a deep bass tone and playing exotic instruments. But all of this is not some bizarre rock concert: it is the most solemn ritual of the Gelugpa school of Vajrayana (also called Tibetan) Buddhism, the Kalachakra Initiation, and it is being administered by the most revered of Tibetan Buddhist monks—the **Dalai Lama**.

In front of the Dalai Lama, who is sitting on the raised dais, is a large complex picture which has been painstakingly crafted out of many different colored sands. This picture may take several weeks to construct since the grains of sand often have to be placed one or two at a time by monk-artists who spend their whole lives mastering the intricate design. This is the Kalachakra *Mandala*. It represents a sort of road map of the entire universe as it is understood by Vajrayana Buddhists. Its purpose is to help lead the individual to *Nirvana*.

Tibetan Buddhists believe that since people have different talents and abilities, each individual must use a different combination of techniques to leave the cycle of birth and death. As in all other Buddhist schools, meditation is seen as a major tool in this quest. But Tibetan Buddhists also believe that Enlightenment can be achieved through the power of ritual. This dual approach sets Tibetan Buddhism apart from other Buddhist schools who feel that ritual is always subordinate to meditation, and that progress toward Enlightenment is gradual over a series of lifetimes. The Tibetan school believes that one can achieve Enlightenment in one lifetime, if one is prepared to take certain risks. The suddenness of Enlightenment in Tibetan Buddhism has given it its other name, *Vajrayana*—the Way of the Thunderbolt.

Initiations are a particular feature of Tibetan Buddhism. The tradition out of which this school developed was *Tantra*. *Tantrism* held that initiation by a *guru* or teacher into particular practices and certain texts was necessary if one was to make progress toward *Nirvana*. Tibetan Buddhists believe that the higher the spiritual attainment of the *guru*, the more effective the initiation. Since the current Dalai Lama is the spiritual head of the Tibetan tradition, many people, both men and women, traveled to New York to receive his initiation. Most of the people attending the Kalachakra ritual do not intend to enter into serious practice and be ordained into the *Sangha*. Rather they believe that the initiation will bear fruit in a future life and create the conditions which will lead to Enlightenment. In a sense, it is future life insurance.

Those who want to deepen their Buddhist practice, through the use of the text and practices that this initiation empowers them to study, have been preparing for it for some time. The way to do this is to undertake the preliminary practices. The actual practices vary somewhat from one Tibetan school to another, but several practices are common to all. The first of these is prostration. Here the practitioner stretches out full length on the floor in front of a shrine to the Buddha and then rises completely to his or her feet again. This practice is to be performed one hundred thousand times.

Also practiced one hundred thousand times is a symbolic offering made for the good of all living beings—not just human beings. The same is true for recitation of the practitioner's *mantra* or sacred formula. All of these practices are regarded as necessary if the practitioner is to develop the essential base of ethical and spiritual purity needed to attempt the difficult and dangerous *Vajrayana* path. The higher initiations that follow these preliminary practices allow the practitioner to undertake specific forms of meditation. Often these involve the use of

Tibetan monks wearing yellow hats perform a ceremony at Quezhang Lamasery, China.

particular *mantras*, mystical chants, or techniques involving the visualization of a special **yidam** or guardian deity as the focus of the practitioner's meditation.

The ritual element of Tibetan Buddhism is particularly evident in the Kalachakra ceremony. Everything in the ceremony is calculated to involve the recipient in the initiation. Rather than deny the body, Tibetan Buddhism believes in using the entire body as a vehicle for salvation. Sweet-smelling incense, bright colors and intricate patterns, the heavy, rhythmic bass of the instruments and the massed choir of monks, all of these are used to slowly lead the practitioner's consciousness out of the world of the senses and into higher realms of reality. This is accomplished through the extensive use of symbols. Here, the *mandala* is of central importance. Even the material from which the *mandala* is constructed is symbolic, representing the temporary nature of human existence. At the end of the ritual, the *mandala* is destroyed and the sand is thrown into the sea or a river, never to be used again. This emphasizes the transient nature of *samsara*.

Many other symbols are used as well. The Dalai Lama and many of the monks hold **dorjes** and **ghantas** with which they perform ritual hand movements called **mudras**. *Dorjes* are small double ended scepters, usually made of bronze, which represent lightning bolts. In turn, these lightning bolts represent both **skillful means**—that is the practice of using all facets of the human existence to gain Enlightenment—and the indestructible, changeless nature of reality. The *ghantas* are hand bells held in the opposite hand which represent the wisdom which the practitioner is attempting to cultivate. Other symbols can be found in Tibetan Buddhism. One of these is the **phurba**, or ritual dagger, which is used to symbolically cut off ignorance. Also used in some rituals are cups made from human skulls and trumpets made from human thigh bones.

These may seem strange or even repellent to European or American eyes, but this need not be the case. Like all Buddhists, the Tibetans believe that all human beings go through an endless series of rebirths. Thus death is neither a unique event nor one to be feared. The body that is left behind is likewise of no particular significance. If it is utilized in a good way, then its former owner will benefit in his or her new life from this use. A good example of this is **sky burial**. Here, the body of the deceased is cut into pieces and laid out for scavengers. After it has been defleshed, the bones are collected, cleaned, and either buried or used to make religious articles. To the Tibetans, giving one's dead body as food to other living creatures and for the making of religious articles is an act of great generosity that benefits all concerned.

| The Roots of Buddhism | 2 |

Indian Religion at the Time of the Buddha

To understand how the various practices and beliefs discussed in the previous chapter came into being, we must first understand the historical development of Buddhism. Buddhism, like most other religions, originated in a particular place at a particular time, and its roots are in forms and ideas that were part of the

 environment in which it developed. It is necessary, therefore, to consider the development of religion in India. India is a very large country that is isolated from the rest of Asia by high mountains and oceans. These features also contribute to its climate. India has what is called a monsoon climate with three distinct seasons, the hot season, the cool season, and the rainy season. During the rainy season, which lasts roughly from May to October, the heavy rainfall severely limits travel through the countryside.

In addition, India is crisscrossed by mountain ranges and rivers that divide it into distinct areas. The most important of these areas at the time of the Buddha was the valley of the Ganges river which flows from west to east across most of northern India. It was here that the great religions of India first arose and flourished. Only later did they spread to the south. In the time of the Buddha, about 500 B.C.E., this area was undergoing a period of vigorous religious development.[1] Of these various

---

[1] The actual dates of the Buddha and the early events which shaped Buddhism are still matters of serious debate among scholars. The dates given in the

intellectual currents, three schools of thought influenced the development of Buddhism: the Vedic religion, the Sramanic movement, and Jainism.

Brahmanism: The Early Indian Religion of Sacrifice

The first and oldest of these movements was the ancient Vedic religion. The Vedas were the sacred books of the Aryans, a people most scholars believe to have come to India from the plains of southern Russia sometime between c. 2000 and 1500 B.C.E. The earliest Aryans spoke a language that was the remote ancestor of present-day English, and which later developed in India into **Sanskrit**, the sacred language of Hinduism. These seminomadic, cattle-herding tribes came to dominate the indigenous agriculturalists who were already living in India when the Aryans arrived. Aryan society was divided into three main social groups, the priests, warriors, and common people. This social division was known as the **caste** system. Each group was seen as having a particular duty to perform in society and, in later times, when the system became more rigid, could not marry or even eat with individuals from the other castes. This was particularly true with respect to the conquered non-Aryans. These people made up a fourth caste. Religion was the particular province of the priestly class, the **brahmins**, who were seen as the highest of the castes. The oldest religious document that has come down to us from the Aryans, the *Rig Veda*, shows us that their religion was not static. Rather, it was a living entity that changed and developed over time.

Initially, the Aryans seem to have practiced a very straightforward religion in which the key element was sacrifice. The gods, such as Indra the warrior king of the gods and Agni the god of fire, were believed to be the personification of nature's power. The Aryans believed that the gods were motivated by more or less the same things that motivated humans. Thus sacrifices

---

following chapters are those to which the majority of scholars adhere. But even these dates are approximate (approximate dates are preceded by the sign "c.").

were seen as a kind of commercial transaction in which the person who was offering the sacrifice was "trading" something to the god. In return, the sacrificer hoped to receive some favor, usually of a material nature, such as long life, many sons, or success in war.

Performing the sacrifice was the province of the priestly class. In the earliest portions of the *Rig Veda*, written between c. 1500 and c. 1000 B.C.E., these sacrifices seem to have been relatively simple affairs. A cow or some other animal was slaughtered and the god was invited to descend from the sky in order to partake of the subsequent feast with his earthly worshipers. As time went on, however, the sacrificial rites became more and more complex. By the time of the Buddha in c. 500 B.C.E., some of these rituals could extend over as much as a year and require a staggering outlay of wealth and the employment of a large number of priests.

This had two effects on the development of **Brahmanism**, the term used for the later phase of Vedic religion. First, it meant that the poorer and less powerful members of Aryan society were excluded from many of the more elaborate rituals of their religion. They simply could not afford to perform the complex and expensive rituals. Moreover, the conquered peoples of the land were also excluded from the sacrifices. In effect, they were completely cut off from the religion of their conquerors. Second, it allowed the brahmin priests to wield more and more power within Aryan society.

We can see this development in the next layer of Brahmanic texts, written between c. 1200 and 900 B.C.E. Here the focus of attention is not on stories of and hymns to the gods, as it was in the *Rig Veda*. Rather, the major theme of these three books is the correct performance of the sacrifices. These sacrifices had become so cumbersome that instruction books for the performers of the sacrifices had become necessary, and that, in essence, is what these texts were. Mixed in with these instructions, however, we begin to see the start of a long Indian tradition of religious and philosophical speculation. These speculations centered on the creation of the world, the nature of reality, and more pragmatic questions such as the role of the sacrifices in maintaining cosmic order.

The Sramana Movement: The Rise of Religious Speculation and Individual Effort

As time went on, the priests became more and more convinced that their actions were not only pleasing to the gods, they actually *compelled* the gods to grant the desired results. As one might expect, the brahmins now saw themselves as the preeminent

Shiva is one of many Hindu gods. Buddhism was partially a revolt against the complicated and expensive rituals required to serve these gods.

members of Aryan society, since their ritual actions generated the forces that sustained and moved the cosmos. But other groups in Aryan society were considering the same basic religious questions as the brahmins. Their conclusions were radically different from those of the priestly class. These other thinkers, who seem to have lived between c. 900 and 600 B.C.E., were known collectively as the **Sramanas**.

Instead of viewing the sacrifice as concrete ritual action, the *Sramanic* thinkers believed that the sacrifice was a symbolic and allegorical representation of internal transformation. Thus each element of the sacrifice corresponded to some internal attitude or action on the part of the individual. Initially, *Sramanic* philosophy was relatively material in nature. For example, the motivating principle that sustained life, *prana*, was seen as being identical with the breath and, by extension, with the wind. But *Sramana* thinking quickly progressed beyond these rather crude beginnings and gave rise to some concepts which have been central to Indic religious thinking ever since.

Primary among these ideas is the concept of **atman** and **Brahman**. In their speculation about religion, the *Sramanic* thinkers explored many avenues, as we can see from their philosophical books, the **Upanishads**. The *atman* was pure spirit, unchanging and immortal. In turn, the *atman* was a fragment of *Brahman*, the spiritual force that created and sustained the universe. Since *atman* was immortal, the *Sramanic* philosophers wondered what happened to it at death when the physical body ceased to exist. The early Aryans had believed in a sort of heaven, but the *Sramanic* philosophers rejected this idea in favor of the concept of **reincarnation**.

Reincarnation, the idea that human beings die and are reborn in a new physical body continuously, soon came to be an accepted idea in all of the Indic religions. But at the same time, it raised other philosophical problems. These problems became even greater when a shift occured in *Sramanic* thinking sometime between c. 800 and 600 B.C.E. Before this period, the Aryan people held a generally positive attitude toward life and the created world. Life was seen as being essentially good. After

c. 800 B.C.E., however, the Indic worldview became distinctly pessimistic. Life's pleasures were viewed as fleeting and ultimately unsatisfying. When this new appraisal of the human condition became widespread, the process of reincarnation came to be regarded as a burden and something to be avoided.

Another idea that developed at this time was the concept of *karma*. This concept hinged on the simple premise that all actions had reactions. Good actions had good reactions, and bad actions had bad reactions. But what about those individuals who performed good acts, but suffered nevertheless? Or those who were exceptionally evil, but prospered anyway? Here again, reincarnation provided an answer. If the effects of one's actions were not felt in this life, they would be felt in one's next life or even the life after that. This allowed Indic religions to sidestep the Problem of Evil. When seen from the perspective of *karma* and reincarnation, bad things happened to good people as a result of previous bad actions on the part of the individual. Moreover, those who acted improperly would suffer from their actions, if not in this life then at a later date.

All of these new philosophical concepts shaped the ideas and goals of the *Sramanic* religious practitioners, who tended, by and large, to be from the non-brahmin classes of Indian society. If human beings were constantly reborn into a fundamentally unsatisfactory world, then the most desirable goal available to human beings was to achieve *moksha*, deliverance from the constant cycle of birth and death. This could be accomplished through the reunion of the individual *atman* with the universal *Brahman*. But how was this to be achieved? Here views differed, but most *Sramanas* agreed that the only way that the *atman* could be reunited with *Brahman* was through practices designed to weaken the body's hold on the *atman*. These practices, called collectively asceticism, could include such things as fasting, celibacy, and going without sleep or even clothing. This asceticism generated *tapas*, a sort of spiritual power which could be used to break out of the endless cycle of life and reunite the *atman* with *Brahman*. We know from the Buddhist scriptures such as the *Digha-nikaya* that many of these

Sramanas practiced very severe austerities. In addition to fasting and going without sleep, they also vowed to do things such as never to sleep lying down, never to stay in a house, never to wear any clothes, to hold an arm above their head for a fixed number of years, to stand on one leg for ten years, and so forth. Such heroic deeds of asceticism are not merely a feature of the past in India; they still take place today.

The Jains: Individual Effort Within an Organized Religious Fraternity

The third major influence on the Buddha's thinking was a group of ascetics known as the **Jains**. Unlike the *Sramanas* and the brahmins, the Jains have a clearly defined founder, Mahavira (c. 580–500 B.C.E.), who was believed to be the last in a line of 24 such Jain leaders. Mahavira was a member of the warrior class (some stories make him a prince). Despite being married and having a son, he decided to abandon his pleasant secular life in order to attempt to escape the cycle of reincarnation. He was a notable ascetic who is said to have achieved Enlightenment and been freed from the worldly cycle. After his Enlightenment, he began to gather his followers into an organized fraternity with a clearly defined program that would lead them to Enlightenment themselves. This program was centered on the key concept of *ahimsa*.

Briefly put, the Jain understanding of *ahimsa*, non-violence, was a direct outcome of their understanding of *karma*. *Karma*, for the Jains, was an actual substance, a sort of sticky residue that weighted the *atman* down and prevented it from rising to the top of the universe where it would escape rebirth. *Karma* accumulated as the result of bad actions, the most serious of which was taking life. Everything, held the Jains, contained a life force. Indeed many things, such as animals and human beings, had more than one such life force. Thus it became imperative for the Jains to minimize the damage that they did to these living beings, since harming living beings was the easiest way of accumulating bad *karma*. The Jains were the first group in India to advocate vegetarianism rather than slaughtering animals for food. But the abstention from accumulating fresh *karma* was not, in itself, sufficient to ensure escape from the cycle of birth and death. One needed to "burn off" the *karma* that had accumulated before one's realization of the truth. Only then could one achieve release from the circle of birth and death.

The Buddha and His Message

The Life of the Buddha

At first, it appears that we have a considerable amount of information concerning the life of Siddhartha of the clan Gautama of the Sakya kingdom, or as he is better known to history, the Buddha or Awakened One (c. 560–480 B.C.E.). But such an assumption would be unwise. The earliest coherent biography of the Buddha, the *Buddhacarita*, was written by Asvaghosa around 100 C.E. Previous to this our knowledge of the Buddha's life can only be reconstructed from stray references in the Buddhist scriptures. Also found in the scriptures are a type of literature called **Jatakas**.

The *Jatakas* describe the lives of the Buddha before his last incarnation and Enlightenment. While these tales provide us with little or no "hard" data about the historical Buddha, they are very important sources for understanding Buddhist ethical and metaphysical doctrines. Consequently, their influence is still felt today in many Buddhist communities. In addition, we should recognize that the life story of the Buddha as we now have it is in itself a stylized account. When one looks at the biography of the other great religious leader of the period, Mahavira, one can see a very similar story. These stories draw on a common pattern of Indian religious biography. The aim of such biography is not so much the recounting of the factual life of the individual as the presentation of that person as an embodiment of a cosmic truth.

The Buddha is believed to have been born in northeastern India in the town of Lumbini, just inside the border of Nepal, in

The Buddha's Disciples

ALL RELIGIONS which have an historical founder have faced a serious problem on the death of this founder. Those religions that have managed to overcome the problem are those where a number of able disciples existed to take up the founder's work. This was the case in Buddhism as well. Indeed, a number of the figures still seen on Buddhist altars are those of these disciples.

The Buddha's favorite disciple seems to have been Sariputra. Born a Brahmin and supposedly an able spokesman for the Hinduism of his time, Sariputra was converted to Buddhism after he and the Buddha debated the relative merits of their respective systems. With his considerable talents now at the disposal of Buddhism, Sariputra travelled around India and was said to have accounted for many of the converts to the new religion. The obvious successor to the Buddha, he is said to have died a few months before his teacher. Today, he is venerated as the personification of wisdom. Sariputra's friend Mahamaudgalyana, who joined the Buddhist Order with him, is also venerated. His particular claim to fame is his supposed supernatural powers.

The monk who is responsible for the continuance of the Buddhist Order on the Buddha's death is Mahakasyapa. Renowned for his asceticism and moral strictness, Mahakasyapa is said to have been the convener of the First Buddhist Council c. 480 B.C.E. It was at this council that the key texts of Buddhism were agreed upon, and the future direction of Buddhism set. Mahakasyapa is also held by Chinese and Japanese Buddhists to be the founder of Zen. His statue is usually found to the right of the image of the Buddha in Zen monasteries.

To the left of the Buddha image is the statue of the second leader of the Zen school, Ananda. He is greatly respected as the personal attendant of the Buddha. When the Buddha, who seems to have been his cousin, died, Ananda was the only monk able to recite all of the Buddha's discourses verbatim.

560 B.C.E. His father, Suddhodana, was described as the king of this region, and so the Buddha was born not into the priestly class but into the warrior/ruler class. His mother, Mahamaya, was said to have conceived without human intervention, and she seems to have died seven days after the birth of her son who was raised by his aunt. Shortly after his birth, according to the customs of his people, a brahmin priest was consulted so that the young Siddhartha's horoscope could be cast and his future charted. The brahmin then informed his father that the young prince would become either a great king or a great religious leader.

His father, wishing his son to follow him on the throne, decided to carefully shield the boy from experiencing any of the disappointments and disillusionments of the world. Consequently, the Buddha was raised in a privileged and pampered environment, being taught the skills that he would need to be a secular ruler. In due course, the Buddha married his cousin Yasodhara and they had a son, Rahula. Despite living in the lap of luxury, however, the future Buddha came to wonder about the world beyond the palace gates.

One day, at the age of about 29, he told his charioteer that he wanted to go out and see the city. This desire was immediately communicated to the king, who asked the young prince to postpone his outing for a day. During this time, he arranged for all unpleasant reminders of human mortality, such as the infirm and the elderly, to be hidden from his son's sight. Unfortunately for his plans, he missed one old man. The prince, having never seen old age, asked his charioteer what was wrong with the old man. He was informed that it was only the inevitable onset of old age. Disturbed by this, the Buddha made further trips outside without the knowledge of his father, and during these outings encountered sickness and death as well. But on his final trip into the world as a prince, he also encountered a wandering holy man. When he inquired about him, he was told that this was someone who had escaped the evils of the world. Deeply impressed, prince Siddhartha decided to go and do likewise.

In the middle of the night, he kissed his sleeping wife, Yasodhara, and child goodbye. Saddling his favorite horse, he rode away from his life in the secular world forever. At first, he practiced a life of extraordinary austerity similar to that of Mahavira. He wandered the countryside naked in all sorts of weather, fasted continually, did not bath, went without sleep, and in general performed the *tapas* that were common to the *Sramanas* of the period. He also seems to have studied under two famous meditation teachers of the time, Arada Kalama and Udraka Ramaputra, whose names are familiar to us from other religious literature of the period. From these teachers, the Buddha learned how to enter the trance states that mark the practice of *Yoga* even to this day. He did not, however, attain the religious insight that he hoped for. Consequently, he redoubled his severe asceticism, determined to achieve Enlightenment.

One day, as he meditated on the burning sands beside the Ganges river, he came to his first major conclusion, namely that the way of severe asceticism did not work. Just then a passing village woman called Sujata, believing him to be a supernatural being, offered him food and he ate it. This effectively ended the Buddha's period of extreme asceticism. Now the Buddha recast his search for Enlightenment within what he later termed "the middle way." By this, he meant moderation in all things. One should eat a sufficient amount to maintain one's health but not too much. One should take enough rest but not too much. This path of moderation was a radical departure from the religious practices of the times.

Despite this new regime, however, the Buddha still had not found his way out of *samsara*, the cycle of birth and death. Determined to do so, he sat down to meditate under a Bo tree at Bodh Gaya, a small village in what is now Bihar in India. He swore an oath that he would not get up until he either gained Enlightenment or died. On the full moon night of May in c. 525 B.C.E., he achieved Enlightenment. When he arose, he was no longer Prince Siddhartha Gautama of the Shakyas, but the Buddha, He Who Has Awakened.

After spending many days in meditation, the Buddha was moved by compassion for suffering humanity. Although he could now enter *Nirvana*, he decided to remain in the world in order to communicate his insight to others. Over the next 45 years, the scriptures tell us, he preached his new message of salvation and gathered a large following of disciples. These disciples he organized into the Buddhist monastic order, the *Sangha*, possibly on the model of the Jains. The Buddha developed a complex code of rules, called the *Vinaya*, by which members of the *Sangha* lived their lives. He also explained his teachings in a series of talks to his disciples. These talks are collectively called the **Sutras.**

The *Vinaya* and the *Sutras*, along with a third group of texts, the **Abhidharma** or philosophical texts, make up the sacred scripture of early Buddhism, known collectively as the **Tripitika**. The core of the *Sutras* and the *Vinaya* comes from the time of the Buddha. Later additions to these scriptures, and the development of the *Abhidharma* literature, represent attempts to clarify certain passages and to work out the implications of the early scriptures to their fullest extent. In the early years of Buddhism, these texts were memorized by monks and passed on to their students from one generation to another. It is not until some 400 years after the death of the Buddha that they were first written down. The oldest copies of the scriptures that have come down to us are written in **Pali**, a spoken language of central India at, or just after, the time of the Buddha.

Written in the language of the common people, these texts were much more accessible than the scriptures of the brahmins which were written in Sanskrit, an older Aryan language which most people no longer spoke or understood. This use of the vernacular language was no doubt one factor in the rapid spread of Buddhism throughout north India before the Buddha's death at the age of 80 in c. 480 B.C.E. This emphasis on communicating the core ideas of Buddhism in everyday language is still an important characteristic of Buddhism. When Buddhism began to spread across Asia, one of the first things that the missionary monks did was to translate the scriptures into the language of the people among whom they found themselves.

ART FOCUS

Image of the Buddha

TODAY, WE ASSOCIATE THE BUDDHA with the many statues and paintings of him that have been produced over the centuries. It comes as something of a surprise, therefore, to learn that this was not always the case. Early Buddhist art did not contain pictures of the Buddha. Instead, the Buddha was symbolically represented through the picture of an elephant, a footprint, an umbrella, or other images. Nor were there Buddhist temples at this early period. Many art historians believe that it was not until after 300 B.C.E. that Buddhist artists began to produce actual rather than symbolic depictions of the Buddha. It was at this date that Indian artists came in contact with Greek artists from the West. These artists were accustomed to producing lifelike artistic representations, not only of everyday people but of the gods as well. Since the earliest statues of the Buddha are from the northwest regions of India where the Greek and Indian worlds met, there seems much to support this idea.

While some early portraits of the Buddha were done in a completely realistic manner, Buddhist artists soon developed their own ideas about how the Buddha should be portrayed. In a primarily illiterate society, Buddhist art formed a very useful adjunct to the oral teachings of the itinerant preacher-monks. Very quickly the statues and paintings of the Buddha became stylized teaching tools. Each representation had to have the so-called "Thirty-Three Auspicious Features." These were physical marks which pointed to the supernatural origins and superior spiritual development of the Buddha. In addition, the Buddha was often depicted as much larger than other figures in a work of art in order to emphasize his spiritual superiority.

Even though this formalized canon of Buddhist art penetrated throughout the Buddhist world, there was still a great deal of scope for local genius. Thus, as Buddhism spread, new styles of portraying the Buddha developed as well. In Thailand, for example, poses of the Buddha walking, rather than sitting, were popular and the willowy, liquid composition of these Buddha statues cannot be mistaken for any other style. Likewise, in China, Korea, and Japan, the image of the Buddha evolved to fit the tastes of these cultures. It is from these styles that we get the impression of the heavy-set, well-fleshed Buddha. In Sri Lanka a realistic style evolved which led to many temples having large dioramas of lifelike figures which recount various scenes from the life of the Buddha.

*Katra Buddha,
Indian, early
first century C.E.*

The Buddhist Path

The Buddha based his analysis of the human condition on three
basic perceptions which he termed the **Three Marks of
Existence**. The first of these marks or characteristics of the
nature of human existence, and the foundation of the entire
Buddhist religious system, is impermanence (**anitya**). Everything, said the Buddha, is in a state of flux. Nothing in the material world is permanent. Things may give the impression of
being permanent, but that is only an illusion. Given enough
time, everything, mountains, seas, the heavens, and especially
human beings, will change and eventually cease to be—they are
impermanent. The second mark of existence, unsatisfactoriness
(**duhkha**, literally "suffering") arose from this impermanence.
All things which were not permanent were, in the Buddha's way
of thinking, unsatisfactory. To place one's trust in any material
thing was pointless and doomed to failure. The third mark of
existence also derived from the first. This was the idea of **anatman**. Human beings, said the Buddha, did not have a permanent
soul (**atman**). For the Buddha, the human being was a compos-
ite being made up of an ever shifting cloud of physical and mental components. Thus to talk about an eternal "kernel" of the
human being that persisted after death was, in the Buddha's
opinion, utterly false. Certain traits and characteristics might
persist from one life to another, but not the personality *per se*.
Moreover, all seemingly concrete phenomena in the world were
really the results of constantly shifting factors. This idea, called
by the Buddhists *pratitya-samutpada*, meant that almost nothing had any existence in itself independent of previous causes.

But the Buddha went on from this somewhat pessimistic
understanding of the human condition to suggest that there
was a way out of the human predicament. This way was the **Four
Noble (i.e. Great) Truths**. The first of these was that life was, in
its essence, unsatisfactory. The second of these was the idea
that the unsatisfactoriness of the world stemmed from the constant cravings (*trsna*, literally "thirst") which arose in the
human being and from ignorance (*avidya*) of the true nature of
reality. The third Noble Truth was that this need not be the fate

of all human beings, and that there was a way to cease being enslaved to this unsatisfactory world. The final Noble Truth was that the way to cessation of bondage to the world lay in the Eightfold Path. The eight components of this path of liberation were 1) right (i.e. correct or proper) viewpoint, 2) right intention, 3) right speech, 4) right actions, 5) right livelihood, 6) right effort, 7) right mindfulness, and 8) right concentration. Here, encapsulated in a very few easy to remember steps, lies the entire Buddhist plan for salvation.

When examined more closely this list divides into three separate parts. The first part, right viewpoint and right intention, relates to the underlying core of one's understanding of the nature of reality. In order for his program of liberation to be effective, the Buddha knew that its practitioners had to change fundamentally the way in which they perceived the world. This was the purpose of right viewpoint, an orientation away from the understanding of the world as made up of material things that were acted upon, and toward an understanding of the world as a series of constantly changing and interacting processes. From this new understanding of the world came the second step on the Eightfold Path, right intention. This was achieved when the individual decided that the Buddhist analysis of existence was correct and determined to follow the Buddhist plan for salvation. This meant acting in a benevolent, non-harmful manner and practicing the steps of the Eightfold Path.

The next three steps on the Eightfold Path were designed to take the insights gained from the first two steps and to put them into practice in the world. Right speech, as its name implies, was based on a proper use of speech, but it really involves the entire way in which human beings interact with one another. Thus one was enjoined not to lie, not to slander, not to backbite, not, in a word, to say (or presumably even think) anything which would upset or cause pain to another. This intention of not harming another was also played out in the next step of the Path, right action. Here one chose not to steal, not to kill, not to use sex improperly (a rule which had different applications depending on whether one was a monk or not), not to use intoxicating substances, and generally not to do anything which would harm or upset another. The fifth step, right livelihood, was closely allied to the fourth in that it forbade making one's living by any means which would cause harm, such as being an arms dealer, selling drugs, being a butcher, and so forth. The sixth step on the Eightfold Path is quite simple. It is right effort. The Buddha did not believe that the absence of wrongdoing was sufficient to lead one to ultimate success. Rather, one needed to put forth a positive effort, both in doing good and in practicing religious exercises.

It is only when we come to the last two steps of the Eightfold Path, right mindfulness and right concentration, that we encounter actions that we would consider explicitly religious. Right mindfulness was a uniquely Buddhist spiritual exercise that consisted of carefully keeping track of one's own thoughts and actions. This practice was generally restricted to monks and nuns. The practitioner of right mindfulness was urged "when walking, be aware that you are walking; when sitting, be aware that you are sitting; when breathing, be aware that you are breathing." This is the first stage in the Buddhist's effort to "wake up," and formed the foundations for the last step on the Eightfold Path, right concentration, or as we would put it, right meditation.

Buddhist meditation can be further broken down into two categories. The first of these is **samadhi**. *Samadhi* literally means "calm abiding," that is to say calming the mind. If one practices mindfulness, one of the first things that one observes is that the mind is in constant movement. Our thoughts bubble up unbidden and float through the mind in a constant whirlpool of agitation. In order for one to penetrate more deeply into the true nature of reality, the Buddhists believe that it is first necessary to calm this fountain of thought. This is the goal of practices designed to induce *samadhi*. The second step in this process is to practice **vipasana**, or "insight" meditation. It is through the practice of this form of meditation that the final realization of the nature of reality can be made, and freedom from the endless cycles of *samsara* gained.

The Early Historical Development of Buddhism | 3

The Development of Buddhism in South Asia

As with most religions, the early years of Buddhism are shrouded in obscurity. One thing is certain, however, and that is that the *Sangha*, the Buddhist order of monks, survived the physical death, or *Parinirvana*, of the Buddha. But the period between that event and the reemergence of Buddhism into the light of history around 250 B.C.E. is somewhat unclear. Buddhist tradition holds that there was a meeting, or council, held immediately following the Buddha's death. The major concern of this meeting was to stabilize the Buddhist scriptures by coming to an agreement as to what were the accepted scriptures as spoken by the Buddha. For a variety of reasons, no  such agreement seems to have been reached, although there was some general agreement on the basic message of the Buddha. This meant that to a certain extent the interpretation of what was a genuine Buddhist scripture and what was not was left up to the individual Buddhist.

Leaving the canon, that is to say the total collection of Buddhist scriptures, open in this way was to lead to disagreements later in Buddhist history. The Second Buddhist Council at Vaisali in c. 380 B.C.E. met precisely because a dispute arose over interpretations of the Buddhist scriptures. In this case, the problem lay in the interpretation of the monastic rules found in the *Vinaya*. One group, the *Mahasanghikas*, was more open to a relaxed interpretation of the rules, and to the belief that an *arhant*, one who had achieved Enlightenment in this lifetime, could still be subject to human uncertainties and frailties. Their opponents, the *Sthaviras*, or "Elders," who formed the majority of the *Sangha*, were much more rigorous in their interpretation of the received tradition. Unable to resolve their differences, the two groups henceforth went their separate ways. Thus, a century after the death of its founder, Buddhism began to split into different groups.[2]

On the whole, it does not seem that this division within the *Sangha* had any particular effect on the expansion of Buddhism, or on its continued success among the peoples of India. Nor did later splits in the *Sangha* over other interpretations of the *Vinaya*. Eventually, there were to be some 18 schools, or *nikayas*, of Buddhism in early Buddhist India. By 250 B.C.E., Buddhism's popularity in India was extremely high. One of the greatest of India's rulers, Asoka Maurya (c. 280–200 B.C.E.) seems to have given his support to the Buddhist *Sangha*. He is best known for the series of inscriptions he ordered carved in order to promulgate a code of behavior that is Buddhist in tone. These inscriptions are the first tangible evidence of how greatly Buddhism had come to influence Indian life and thought.

In 240 B.C.E., the Third Council of Buddhism was convened in the Mauryan capital city of Pataliputra. Here the assembled Buddhist monks purged the *Sangha* of monks who were not sincere in their religious professions and attempted, once again without success, to promulgate an authoritative version of the Buddhist scriptures. More important for the future of

---

[2] A note must be added here concerning "schism," and its associated term "heresy," in Buddhism. Schism could only take place within the order of monks, since for Buddhists schism meant a disagreement on the manner in which the monastic rules were interpreted. It naturally followed that lay persons were legally incapable of being "schismatic" or "heretical" since they were, by definition, outside this legal framework. It is for this reason that we seldom see wholesale warfare between differing factions in Buddhist history, although sectarianism did have an effect when the ruling class held to one form of Buddhism and the monks to another.

Buddhism, however, was the decision to expand Buddhist missionary efforts outside of India proper. After the fall of the Mauryan Empire, Buddhist influence began to decline in India. But this decline was by no means swift. Buddhist missionary activity continued with notable success, particularly in Sri Lanka. Sri Lankan kings adopted Buddhism as the state religion in c. 200 B.C.E. Likewise, a number of later Indian rulers were attracted to the religion. Notable among these was Kaniska, a king belonging to a nomadic people who had invaded and settled in the Mauryan provinces in Central Asia and northwestern India. It was Kaniska who called the Fourth and last Buddhist Council sometime around 100 C.E. This Council, which is not accepted as being canonical by the Theravada school of Buddhism (the modern descendants of the *Sthavira* party), was yet another doomed attempt to develop an authoritative canon of scripture.

The Rise of Mahayana Buddhism

It is during the period from c. 100 B.C.E. to c. 200 C.E. that we see the development of what was to become the second great expression of Buddhism—**Mahayana**. Mahayana Buddhism was not a single school of thought, but rather a movement which initially gained its identity by distinguishing itself from other movements within Buddhism. Mahayanist tendencies are seen in Buddhism from early times, notably in attempts to emphasize the primacy of the *sutras* over the other two divisions of scripture. Earliest indications that we have for the emergence of a distinct Mahayana tradition date from c. 100 B.C.E.

Three concepts came to dominate this emerging school of thought. The first of these was the idea of **sunyata**. *Sunyata* means emptiness and it was the logical development of the earlier Buddhist concept that the human being did not possess an enduring soul and that all things were conditioned by preexisting conditions (*pratitya-samutpada*). The Mahayanist philosophers took this one step further. Nothing, they said, had

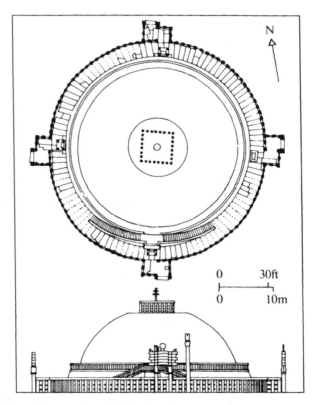

Plan of Great Stupa, Sanchi, third century B.C.E–first century C.E. This is the most remarkable surviving example of the 84,000 Buddhist burial mounds reputedly erected by the emperor Asoka. Its four gates were carefully oriented to the points of the compass.

any independent reality or enduring substance. Things might appear to be solid and self-existing, but with the development of the insight gained through meditation one discovered that this was not so. This insight, in turn, led to Enlightenment.

The second concept that became central to Mahayana thought was the belief that the Buddha's death was only an illusion and that he remains accessible to suffering humanity. According to the believers in Mahayana, only the Buddha's gross material body had died. His subtle material body and "spiritual" self, dwelling on other planes of existence, was still available for consultation to a select few. For these Buddhists, the Buddha was still alive and capable of preaching new truths about the Buddhist religion. Thus, from the first century B.C.E. onward, a new literature claiming to be the direct word of the Buddha arose within the existing Buddhist community. This literature, while taking more notice of lay Buddhists, seems to have been written primarily by monks. Cults arose around each of these new *sutras* with little or no interconnection, each being peculiar to the geographical region in which they originated.

Adherents to these new texts felt themselves to be in direct contact with the Buddha, whether through the medium of the new *sutras* themselves or through the more direct paths of meditation and dreams. They also seem to have held (in contradiction to other segments of the Buddhist community), that these new *sutras*, being direct communications from the Buddha himself, were more worthy of veneration than the *stupas* which contained only the dead remains of the Buddha's material body.

But the concept that was to have the most profound effect on the development of Buddhist thought was that of the **Bodhisattva**. *Bodhisattvas* were beings who had achieved Enlightenment, but had taken a vow that they would continue to be reborn into the world until all beings were saved. Many Buddhists were dissatisfied with the ideal of the *arhant*, the self-motivating and isolated Buddhist practitioner who was solely interested in his own release. Pointing to the example of the Buddha himself, these later thinkers held that if one were truly spiritually evolved, one would be filled with compassion for all other creatures who suffered in *samsara's* cycle of birth and death. Such a being would postpone his or her own entrance to *Nirvana* in order to aid suffering beings.

Thus the emphasis in Buddhism began to shift subtly from primary concentration on the individual self to concentration on all of existence. Moreover, since the *Bodhisattvas'* spiritual development exceeded that of ordinary beings, they possessed powers and abilities far beyond those of the average human being. Thus they could render spiritual and material aid to those who

ART FOCUS

The Growing Role of the Bodhisattva

WITH THE RISE OF MAHAYANA Buddhism, the figure of the *Bodhisattva* became increasingly popular. In time, these figures came to dominate and even eclipse the figure of the Buddha in the mind of many Buddhists. This is not a surprising development for the Buddha was seen as a remote figure—great teacher and worthy of respect, but not available to help his followers in the same way as the *Bodhisattvas*. Since Buddhists were often in need of worldly as well as spiritual aid, the *Bodhisattvas*, who were capable of providing both, took center stage in the minds of many Buddhists. The earliest of these *Bodhisattvas* is Maitreya. He is portrayed as residing in heaven, preparing to be incarnated as this world's next Buddha. Of all the *Bodhisattvas*, he is the only one to be venerated by both Mahayanists and Theravadins.

Of the other *Bodhisattvas* venerated by the Mahayana and Vajrayana schools, the greatest is Avalokitesvara. He is seen as infinitely compassionate and always ready to come to the aid of suffering beings in the material world. Artistic conventions concerning his depiction were soon established. He was depicted as having a thousand eyes to see the troubles of the world and a thousand arms to relieve them. As Buddhism dispersed through Asia, new artistic renderings developed that adapted the images of the *Bodhisattvas* to new environments, sometimes with peculiar results. In the case of Avalokitesvara, he came to be venerated in China as Kuan-yin. But Kuan-yin was portrayed in art as being female! This gender change became the norm throughout the Chinese-influenced cultures of East Asia.

But Avalokitesvara was not the only *Bodhisattva* to be venerated by the Buddhist faithful. Another important figure was that of Manjusri. This *Bodhisattva* was seen as being the embodiment of the Supreme Wisdom to be gained through meditation, and so he is often represented in Buddhist monasteries. But Manjusri is anything but a benign figure. Armed with a sword to cut the bonds of delusion, Manjusri's fierce countenance is a constant reminder of the difficulty inherent in the quest for Enlightenment. Some *Bodhisattvas* have purely local cults. A good example of this is the Japanese cult of Jizo. Jizo is supposed to have taken a vow to save Buddhists from the tortures of Hell. In that capacity, he is particularly venerated as the savior of children, and statues of this *Bodhisattva* are often placed on the graves of children.

A Tibetan bronze statue of Avalokitesvara, the 1000-armed Bodhisattva *of infinite compassion.*

called upon them. It is not surprising, therefore, that great popular devotion developed toward them. The most popular *Bodhisattvas*, such as Avalokitesvara, Manjusri, and Maitreya, came to be venerated almost as gods, and played an increasingly central role in popular devotion as Buddhism spread out of its original Indian homeland.

At first, those who followed these new Mahayanist ideas were a minority in the Buddhist community, and their public behavior did not differ in any significant respect from their non-Mahayana neighbors. It was only later, possibly when they had to compete for declining resources as revived Hinduism began to eat away at their lay support in India, that animosity arose between the two groups. In any case, Mahayana Buddhism was never to dominate the Indian scene. Its real successes were to come elsewhere as Buddhism spread to East Asia.

The Buddhist Mission and the Spread
of Buddhism in East Asia

Originally, Buddhism was brought to China through trade sometime around the beginning of the Common Era. It has generally been held that the first penetration of the new religion into the already ancient civilizations of the east was through the medium of traders from Central Asia, an area which had been strongly influenced by Buddhism since the time of Asoka. However, it seems reasonable to suppose that there may have been an equally important flow of Buddhist culture along the sea routes to Southeast Asia, and from there into southern China at about the same date. Whatever the case, Buddhism did not make a strong initial impression on the Chinese.

The Chinese were quite contented with their own native thought systems, such as Taoism and Confucianism, and were even somewhat repulsed by the emphasis Buddhism placed on renunciation and celibacy. These were concepts which ran counter to established Chinese ideals. All of this changed when the stable political and social system of China began to disintegrate in the second century C.E. In 148 C.E., a Buddhist missionary called An Shih-kao is credited with translating Buddhist scriptures into Chinese for the first time. These translations were not of particularly high quality, since they necessitated the invention of Buddhist terms in Chinese and at first Taoist terms were used to convey Buddhist ideas. This was to lead to some intermixing of Taoist and Buddhist ideas in the Chinese mind. During these earliest days of Buddhism in China, short practical texts and handbooks on meditation, rather than long philosophical dissertations, were the first to be translated.

With the downfall of the Han Dynasty in 220 C.E., China entered a period of political disunity and social disruption that did not end until the rise of the Sui dynasty in 589 C.E. Despite the fact that Chinese dynasties still managed to maintain a foothold in north China, the fortunes of the Chinese began to decline. In 311 C.E., barbarians from the steppes of central Asia swept into China and eradicated Chinese political control of northern China for almost 300 years. This change of political fortunes resulted in the emigration of officials and learned monks from the north to the south, where they finally settled in Chien-k'ang, near the present city of Nanking. There they assisted in the establishment of the Eastern Chin Dynasty and began to play a dominant role in the intellectual life of the area. From the melding of these intellectuals and religious leaders there developed for the first time a Buddhism of the upper classes, or "gentry" Buddhism.

Gentry Buddhism emphasized both Buddhist and Chinese learning, and indulged in philosophical discussions, and literary activities based on a mixture of Taoist and Buddhist ideas. Buddhism also flourished in the newly constituted barbarian states of the north. Here, however, the religion developed along different lines. In the north, Buddhism was a state religion, constituted by, and maintained for, the purposes of the foreign rulers of the land. Monks in north China often played a political as well as a religious role in the state, and were skilled in political and military matters.

The peasants in north China had a very different view of the usefulness of Buddhism. They took to Buddhism because becoming a monk offered a refuge from taxation and conscript labor. Moreover, Buddhism in northern China began to develop ritually in ways which allowed for peasant participation, such as the making of offerings at temples, pilgrimage, and praying to various *Bodhisattvas*. It is from these beginnings that the two separate and often distinct levels of Chinese Buddhism arose. On the one hand, there was a philosophical and meditative Buddhism for the upper classes who could afford to pursue religion in a leisurely manner. On the other, there was a more ritualistic Buddhism with an emphasis on supernatural aid and intervention which appealed to the peasants.

With the rise of the T'ang dynasty in the early 600s C.E., Buddhism entered into its golden age in China. The early rulers of the period patronized the religion strongly, and sent Buddhist monks to India to obtain new scriptures for translation. Thus such famous figures of Chinese Buddhist history as Hsuan-tsang (c. 596–664 C.E.), who traveled overland to India, and I-tsing, who left Canton in 671 C.E. on board a Persian trading vessel, brought new life into Chinese Buddhism. This new flurry of translation was also accompanied by exciting new philosophical developments.

Many of these new developments were uniquely Chinese in their orientation. Four of the most important of these new schools of Buddhist philosophy were T'ien-t'ai, Hua-yen, Ch'an (Zen), and Pure Land Buddhism. Although all of these schools agreed with the basic precepts of Buddhism as expounded by the Buddha, their understanding of these precepts was conditioned by Mahayana viewpoints and native Chinese philosophy. The T'ien-t'ai School seems to have been originated about 550 C.E. It takes its name from the mountain monastery founded by Hui-ssu (515–67 C.E.). This school, which had as its major text the **Lotus Sutra**, took an equal interest in meditation and doctrinal analysis. T'ien-t'ai developed an incredibly complex philosophical system aimed at integrating all of the Buddhist philosophical schools into a harmonious whole. From this developed an equally elaborate system of meditation.

The Hua-yen or Flower Garland School (fl. c. 650–750 C.E.), was mainly concerned with philosophical analysis. Starting with the concept of *pratitya-samutpada*, this school held that all phenomena were interdependent and interpenetrating. From this, Hua-yen thinkers developed a highly complex metaphysical system that greatly influenced the philosophical development of the schools that followed it.

Ch'an or Zen Buddhism developed in a somewhat different direction from the heavily philosophical schools that we have just discussed. This school held that the core of Buddhism lay not in philosophy or text study, but in direct experience of Ultimate Reality. This was to be achieved through a rigorous program of meditation. Rather than depending on large tracts of communally owned land, as did the older and more established monastic orders, Ch'an monks wandered from place to place relying on the charity of individuals and on their own labor for support.

Equally important was the development of Pure Land Buddhism. This school or schools, all based to some degree on the Buddhist scriptures titled the **Pure Land Sutras**, held that human effort was not sufficient to achieve salvation given the present degenerate nature of the world. It was therefore necessary to petition supernatural aid from *Bodhisattvas* or Buddhas who lived in other universes, the "Pure Lands." These Pure Lands had not degenerated, as our world had, because of the death of this universe's Buddha. Such Buddhas, and in particular the Buddha Amida, were seen as sympathetic beings who would, if the petitioner called their name with perfect faith, cause them to be reborn in the Pure Lands where the attainment of *Nirvana* was assured. Since this form of Buddhism did not require lengthy periods of meditation, but rather individual acts of piety, it was far more suited to the physically difficult life of the peasant than the meditative and philosophical Buddhism of the upper classes.

Both the hearty individualism of Ch'an and the widespread appeal of Pure Land Buddhism were to stand these schools in good stead during the time that followed. Despite support from the early T'ang emperors, the later rulers of this dynasty turned against Buddhism. There were a number of reasons for this. One was that the T'ang emperors believed they were descended from Lao Tzu, the founder of Taoism, and consequently they increasingly came to favor the Taoists. Another reason was that many people who joined the Buddhist monastic orders were not motivated by sincere religious faith. Rather, they desired the numerous material benefits that such membership conferred and, still living a worldly life, brought disrepute on the very religion that they had promised to uphold. But perhaps the most important reason for the later T'ang repression of Buddhism had to do with property.

Many individuals believed that if they donated their goods and land to the various Buddhist monasteries, they would be assured of a good future rebirth. Since the Buddhist orders were exempt from taxes, this donated property, and the revenues which it could generate for the state, was effectively lost to the government. No government can function with declining tax revenues. In 845 C.E., a strongly Confucian official petitioned the throne to suppress the Buddhist monasteries and purge the priesthood of unworthy monks. The government quickly moved to disband the monasteries. This was disastrous for those Buddhist schools which were primarily monastic, but for Ch'an and Pure Land Buddhism, which were not monastically based, it made very little difference. The peasants continued to patronize these two forms of Buddhism. But the golden age of Chinese Buddhist philosophy was over, never to come again. Buddhism in China now entered a period of slow decline. Still practiced in the countryside, its practices began to become more and more tinged with magic, and less and less concerned with salvation.

The Beginnings of Buddhism in Japan and Korea

At the height of its prestige, Chinese Buddhism was in a favorable position to disseminate itself. T'ang China was the undisputed center of world civilization and was a magnet that drew the other countries of East Asia to it. Consequently, ships carrying Japanese envoys, and ambassadors from the various courts of Korea, constantly made their way to the imperial Chinese capital of Ch'ang-an. From there, they returned to their homelands laden not only with examples of Chinese art and technologies, but with new, and in some cases revolutionary, religious ideas. This is not to say that Buddhism did not penetrate these cultures previous to the eighth century C.E. There is significant evidence to show that Buddhism had, in one form or another, penetrated the Korean peninsula in the second or third century C.E. Indeed, it was from there that it passed on to Japan in the early part of the fifth century. But it was the new strands of Buddhist tradition which had developed in T'ang China, and which were to be further refined in Korea and Japan, that were to become identified with those countries.

Korea and Japan were at this time undergoing significant political changes. They were moving away from local autonomies toward more centralized forms of government. In Korea, the three kingdoms of Paekche, Koguryo, and Silla were locked in a battle to the death for control of the peninsula. When Silla eventually triumphed in 668 C.E., the new central government wanted to synthesize the various Buddhist schools into a single, state-controlled church. During this period of adjustment, Korean Buddhist philosophers created some of the most innovative philosophical speculations that the religion has ever produced. Strongly supported by Silla and its successor states in Korea, Buddhism grew strongly until the thirteenth century. Eventually, the Korean form of Zen, Son, came increasingly to dominate Korean Buddhism. But other philosophies such as Neo-Confucianism began to thrive in opposition to Buddhism, and to receive state support. This, in addition to frequent foreign invasions and natural catastrophes, led to a decline in Buddhism's prestige until the present century.

Similar developments took place in Japan. Originally frowned upon by the Japanese as an unnecessary foreign import, Buddhism rapidly became an established organ of the Japanese state. The emperor and his court were not at first interested in the finer points of Buddhist doctrine, rather they held the somewhat superstitious viewpoint that Buddhist rituals provided their land with better protection from natural disasters and evil spirits than did their own Shinto deities. It was not until the late eighth century, when the two great reformers Saicho (767–822 C.E.), who established Tendai (the Japanese form of T'ien-t'ai), and Kukai (774–835 C.E.), the founder of the ritualistic Tantric Shingon school, returned from China with fresh approaches to the religion that Buddhism began to be understood as a religion and not as magic. Moreover, it was not until somewhat later that the common people began to be drawn to the religion in its Pure Land form as taught by Honen Shonin (1133–1212 C.E.) and his disciple Shinran (1173–1262 C.E.).

By the thirteenth century, other changes had begun to take place in Japanese Buddhism as well. The reformer Nichiren (1222–82 C.E.) had begun to preach an ultranationalist form of Buddhism which held that Japan had become the true spiritual home of the religion. Meanwhile, as Japan descended deeper and deeper into civil war, the emerging warrior classes came to espouse the austere tenets of Zen Buddhism as being best suited to the perilous and precarious lives that they led. Thus, little by little, Buddhism became associated with patriotism and national pride in Japan. This was to have significant effects on the country in the twentieth century.

Tibet and the Development of Vajrayana Buddhism

The development of Vajrayana Buddhism is intimately intertwined with the development of the country of Tibet. In a very real sense, it is amazing that anyone lives in Tibet, let alone prospers as the Tibetan peoples have done. A high, rocky, dry, and desolate region, Tibet has few natural resources to attract human inhabitants. Nor does it occupy a particularly strategic geographical position. Nevertheless it has, from very early times, been the home of nomadic herding peoples. Sometime around 600 C.E. , a lineage of kings arose in central Tibet around the city of Lhasa who were able to unite the Tibetan plateau under their rulership. The first and greatest of these was Songtsen Gampo (c. 609–49 C.E.). To cement his position of authority and improve foreign relations, this king married two wives, one from Nepal to the south and one from imperial China to the north and east. Both of these wives were Buddhist and no doubt this contributed to the spread of Buddhism in Tibet. More important than this, however, was the fact that as Tibet became more unified, the kings of Lhasa found that the old religion, *Bon-po*, could not contribute to their political ambitions to the same degree as could Buddhism.

In addition, Tibet was coming to look beyond its own borders for the first time. During Songtsen Gampo's reign, envoys were dispatched to India where they modified the existing Sanskrit script for use in writing Tibetan (no small feat given that the Sanskrit script is phonetic and Tibetan is a tonal language akin to Chinese). No doubt enterprising Buddhist missionaries were trekking up the passes of the Himalayas from the other direction, and over the eastern mountains from China.

The earliest arrival of these missionaries is shrouded in the mists of time, but legend attributes the establishment of Buddhism in Tibet to one particular holy man, Padmasambhava, who supposedly came to Tibet sometime in the seventh century C.E. Padmasambhava emerges from these early legends as a larger than life figure possessing awesome magical power which he had acquired through severe austerities, secret rituals, and prolonged meditation. Credited with subduing the dangerous and violent gods of the mountains, he is also said to have been responsible for the building of the Jokhang, the first Buddhist temple, in Lhasa during the reign of Songtsen Gampo.

The arrival of Buddhism is more clearly evident in the accounts of the mission of Shantarakshita. Invited to Tibet by the second of the Great Religious Kings, Trisong Detsen (c. 704–97 C.E.), this Indian Tantric master built the Samyé, the other great early temple of Buddhism in Tibet. It was here between 792 and 794 C.E. that the direction of Tibetan Buddhism was decided for all time. These years were the period of the so-called Great Debate between Kamalasila, the representative of the Indian Tantric form of Buddhism, and the Ch'an Buddhist monk Ho-shang Mahayana from China. After these debates, the Buddhism of Tibet was modeled on Indian Buddhism, particularly in its Tantric form. It is from this period as well that the Tibetans began to invest considerable efforts in retrieving Buddhist texts from India and translating them into their own language. They were so successful at this that many texts which have disappeared from the land of their composition are still available in Tibetan translations.

But all was not smooth sailing for the development of Tibetan Buddhism. The last of the Great Religious Kings, Ralpachen (805–38 C.E.), was a weak ruler and perished at the hands of his brother Langdarma. This new king was no friend of Buddhism and attempted to eliminate Buddhism from Tibet. Despite the fact that he was murdered by a Buddhist monk after a brief reign of only four years in 842 C.E., his tenure on the Tibetan throne marked the end both of the first transmission of Buddhism to Tibet and of its being ruled by secular kings. Here a dark age descends on Tibet for 150 years.

This period ended sometime around 1000 C.E. This time the second transmission of Buddhism to Tibet began not in central Tibet, but in the western part of the country. Here the Buddhist teacher Atisha (c. 982–1054 C.E.) brought new teachings from the university at Vikramashila in India to the region before traveling on to central Tibet. Likewise in eastern Tibet, Tibetans such as Drogma and Marpa (c. 1012–96 C.E.) made the arduous trek to the Indian plains in search of inspired teachers from whom they could learn the latest trends in Buddhism. With this new influx of ideas came a renewed interest in Buddhist practice, and the major schools of Buddhism in Tibet date their foundations from this time.

The oldest of these schools was the Nyingmapa or "Old Ones" school which held that its origins predated this second foundation of Buddhism in the early eleventh century of the Common Era. Unlike the other schools of Tibetan Buddhism, the Nyingmapas allowed their monks to marry and have families. Organized in only the loosest possible manner, the Nyingmapas were primarily individualistic in character and concentrated on local issues such as divination, agricultural rituals, and exorcisms.

The next oldest of the Tibetan schools is the Sakya school which was founded by Konchog Gyalpo (1034–1102 C.E.). This school, named for its principal monastery at Sakya in south-central Tibet, was particularly known for its teaching system, called the Lamdre system (which skillfully interwove the study of Tantra and orthodox Buddhist scriptures), and for its focus on a particular text, the *Hevajra Tantra*. This school rapidly began to influence secular as well as spiritual events, and when one of its head monks became the official teacher of the great Sino-Mongol emperor Kublai Khan, the emperor vested him with the secular rule of the entire country of Tibet, then a province of the Mongol Empire. Thus began the long tradition of Tibet's being ruled by the Buddhist monastic orders. This arrangement continued up to 1951 C.E.

The Kagyu school traces its lineage back to Marpa and his famous pupil Milarepa (1052–1135 C.E.). Both of these teachers were well known for their magical attainments, and Milarepa is recognized as the foremost poet of Tibet. The Kagyu were the first school to establish the concept of the *tulku*. A *tulku* is a highly developed monk, usually the founder of a particular order, who reincarnates and takes up residence in a new body time after time in order to resume his duties as head of his order. In much later times, the Kagyu order was one of the first to recognize the potential for expansion to Europe and America, and a number of famous modern monks such as Chogyam Trungpa and Chuje Akong belonged to this order.

But of all the Tibetan schools, the most famous is that of the Dalai Lama, the Gelugpa or Yellow Hat school. Founded as a reform movement at the beginning of the fifteenth century C.E. by Tsongkhapa (1357–1419 C.E.), the Gelug school soon became the preeminent school of Buddhism in Tibet, and a disciple of Tsongkhapa, Gendun-drup (1391–1474 C.E.) was the first head of the school to be called Dalai Lama. His successors were seen as being, at the same time, his reincarnation and the reincarnation of Avalokiteshvara, the *Bodhisattva* of compassion. In 1642 C.E., the fifth Dalai Lama was appointed ruler of all Tibet, and so things remained until the Chinese drove the present fourteenth Dalai Lama out of Tibet in 1959 C.E.

The Decline of Buddhism in India

The Tantric Vajrayana Buddhism of Tibet represents the last major development of Buddhism in its homeland of India. Buddhism found itself more on the defensive as a now resurgent Hinduism began to assert itself. Before 600 C.E., the worship of the gods Shiva and Vishnu began to displace the numerous schools of Buddhism. This is first evident in the southern part of the subcontinent. Before this date, Buddhism had been a highly regarded tradition in south India which was richly patronized by the Kalabhra rulers of southeast India. But by c. 800 C.E., Buddhism had been, to all intents and purposes, eliminated from this part of India.

However, Buddhism still held on in the northeast of the country, with large flourishing monastery-universities which housed and educated hundreds of monks at a time. Travelers from China such as I-tsing and Hsuan-tsang reported that these Buddhist places of learning drew students from all over southern and eastern Asia. The monarchs of faraway states sent costly gifts earmarked for the maintenance of these elaborate institutions. It was here that the Tantric form of Buddhism evolved, and it was from here that it was exported to Tibet and beyond. In many respects, the Buddhism of the monastery-universities had changed significantly from the rather austere faith expounded by the Buddha. Now a complex ritualism shared space with a highly developed and subtle philosophy, and with an ever expanding canon of scripture. Despite this, Buddhism continued, on the whole, to lose ground to its rivals in India. The reasons for this are not completely clear, but certain factors are evident.

India after 700 C.E. was politically very unstable. With the decline of the Gupta dynasty after 450 C.E. and their immediate successor states, India dissolved into a patchwork of petty warring states. This meant that inevitably the lot of the common folk became more and more difficult. Their overall standard of living declined as a result of higher taxes brought on by wars, and by the damages that they sustained in those wars. This had two results. First, the amount that they could afford to donate to religious causes became considerably less than had been the case in more prosperous times. But perhaps more important than that, they were now looking for immediate religious relief. No longer were they interested in longterm release from the cycle of life and death. Rather they wanted a religion that could provide them with tangible results quickly. All of this meant that peasant donations to the Buddhists began to drop off (although not disappear entirely) as the peasants switched their religious allegiances to the gods of Hinduism.

Even at that, Buddhism continued to limp along. But the final blow fell with the Muslim invasions. These invaders swept out of the northwest inflamed with the dual desire of eliminating idolatry and lining their pockets. The richly endowed Buddhist institutions allowed them to do both. Between 1000 and 1200 C.E., wave after wave of Muslim invaders plundered and sacked these last islands of Buddhist influence in India. Those few monks who had escaped the wholesale slaughter of their brethren emigrated to more hospitable lands. The Buddhist monuments and monasteries were converted to use by Muslims and Hindus, destroyed, or sank through neglect into jungle-shrouded obscurity. It was not until the coming of the British, some 600 years later, that these ruins began to give up their secrets, and not for a further 150 years that Buddhism was to reemerge as a living Indian religion.

The Common Inheritance

As we have seen, Buddhism has spread and developed not only in the land of its birth, but in many other lands as well. Why does Buddhism present such an attractive religious option to so many different cultures? Buddhism is no different from other religions in claiming to possess the means by which to attain that most cherished of human goals—eternal peace. Where Buddhism differs is in its acceptance of a number of alternate methods by which to attain this goal, each suited to different temperaments and conditions. As we have seen in Chapter 2, Buddhism developed a sophisticated worldview very early. At the core of this worldview is what later Western philosophers would define as *angst*, that vague feeling of uneasiness and separateness from the world that often tinges life. This inherent element of human existence, say the Buddhists, is an inevitable part of life that is caused by life's intrinsic instability.

This concept that the universe is unstable is reminiscent of modern physics. The ancient Buddhist philosophers saw the world not as a stable, material, entity, but rather as a constantly changing cloud of interactive forces. The Buddhist analysis of the unsatisfactory and unstable nature of existence is the foundation of a whole way of life. That way of life is based not only on the Buddhist understanding of the nature of reality, but also on their understanding of human fate and the factors that affect it. For the Buddhist, human existence is not a brief excursion between birth and death. It extends endlessly through time and space (for the Buddhists believe that there are an almost limitless number of alternate worlds to this one), and the human being can look forward only to an infinite series of rebirths either in this world or elsewhere.

The driving force behind these lives is *karma*, the iron law of cause and effect that meant that good actions will have good results and evil actions evil ones. This means that there is no hope to be had outside of one's self. Human beings are, in the deepest sense, on their own. No supernatural agency exists that can deliver a person from the round of birth and death. Teachers can only point in the direction that one should go. No amount of personal material success can allow you to buy your way out. This bleak picture is relieved by only one thing. The Buddha has discovered a way out, a way to *Nirvana*. However, different groups of Buddhists interpret this basic Buddhist message in different ways in order to fit differing circumstances.

Theravada: The Life of Discipline
and the Production of Merit

Of the many schools of Buddhism which still exist, the one that is closest to the Buddhism of the Buddha is the Theravada school. Now found only in Sri Lanka, Burma, Thailand, Laos, and Cambodia, the Theravada school holds to the oldest collection of Buddhist scripture—the Pali Canon. If we are to look for a simple phrase to sum up Theravada Buddhism's philosophy of spiritual practice, it would be personal effort. Central to the Buddha's revelatory experience was the realization that release from rebirth came from personal effort. There was no god who could save you, no teacher who could present you with the truth. It was only through personal effort that the nature of reality could be understood and the cycle of birth and death broken. Thus salvation, in the broadest sense of the term, needed to be acquired through the disciplining of the mind and body.

Becoming a Monk

In some Theravadin countries, one becomes a monk for as long as the individual chooses to remain in the order. In other countries, the decision to ordain is permanent (or at least intended to be so). In either case, the process of becoming a monk is a two-fold one. The first part of this process is called *pabbajja* or going forth. In a reenactment of the Buddha's renunciation of his home, the aspiring monk "goes forth" from the life

of a householder to that of a member of the *Sangha*. There is no set age at which this ceremony takes place. Often parents decide to have one of their sons ordained at an early age. This is seen as having two benefits. One is to the new monk's family, who gain merit from his ordination and the second is to the young monk himself. In times past, the monkhood was often the only way to gain the education that led to high government position. Even today, many boys are ordained by their parents in order to receive an education.

The ordination ceremony itself is relatively simple. It takes place at a time that is usually determined through consulting the candidate's horoscope. In addition, the young novice's new status is

announced to the gods and local spirits. The candidate has his head shaved and takes a ritual bath. After this, he takes the Three Refuges and is presented with a set of robes and other things used by monks in their daily life. He is now an official member of the Buddhist Order, and it is from this date that his seniority in the Buddhist Order is calculated. What follows is a period of learning under the supervision of a senior monk. After several years of training, but not before his twentieth birthday, the novice may request the second step in the ordination process. This is the rite of *upasampada*. This ceremony marks the novice's full acceptance into the *Sangha*. After this, the monk may serve as a preceptor to younger monks. He may also serve as a member of monastic government. If a monk should choose to leave the Buddhist Order, he simply does so. There is no formal ceremony involved.

Young ordinands take instruction from a monk at a Buddhist school in Bangkok, Thailand.

From the Buddha's point of view, the most important way to employ one's incarnation as a human being, itself a very rare event, was to strive for Enlightenment. Since this was a very difficult undertaking, it came to be regarded as a fulltime job for people specializing in religion. The first thing that the Buddha did when he began to preach was to establish a set of rules which aspirants to Enlightenment needed to follow. These rules, known collectively as the *Vinaya* or Discipline, covered all aspects of the disciple's life. It still forms the framework within which the modern Buddhist monk lives out his life. These regulations lay out what food the monk can eat and when, what clothes he can wear, who he can have sex with, and many other aspects of his life great and small. Those who follow these rules become known as *bhikkhus* and, in the case of women, *bhikkhunis*. Collectively they make up the *Sangha*, the Buddhist Order, which is the personification of the Buddha's teaching.

It is natural, therefore, that the professional monks and nuns in the *Sangha* came to wield considerable influence in early Buddhist society. While changes in other schools of Buddhism resulted in the *Sangha* being less influential, Theravada Buddhism still gives the monk a very prominent role in society. This is somewhat surprising given the fact that the monks are supposed to have little actual interaction with lay people. As the religion grew, however, this stance modified somewhat. Some monks, termed forest monks, continued to hold to the traditional Buddhist monastic ideal of separation from the laity. Other monks, indeed the majority of modern monks, came to be regarded as village monks. These monks lived on the periphery of the village, and acted as school teachers and local religious advisors to the laity. These were the monks who ministered to everyday people.

Unlike other religions, or other forms of Buddhism for that matter, Theravadin religious rituals for the laity are distinctly austere. Lay groups meet on the day of the new moon and that of the full moon each lunar month. At this meeting, which generally has a monk in attendance, they renew their allegiance to the Buddhist lifestyle by publicly reciting the **Three Refuges** and accepting the **Five Precepts**. They then listen to the monk preach a sermon, which is usually of a formal rather than a spontaneous nature. After this, they may indulge in a brief period of meditation. Seasonal festivals have much the same character and center on events in the life of the Buddha.

From one standpoint, there does not seem to be much here of a religious nature. But this is something of a mistake which arises from a misunderstanding of the religious functions appropriate to different segments of society. For the Theravadin Buddhist, religious exercises such as meditation are not the province of the lay person, they are activities generally reserved for monks. The cultivation of insight, hold these Buddhist lay people, is a fulltime job and one which cannot easily be accomplished in the hurly-burly of the modern world. Thus if one wishes to undertake this type of training, one must dedicate oneself to it completely and renounce the world as the Buddha had done. By so doing, one earns tremendous merit and should therefore be treated with the profoundest respect. In Theravada countries today, it is not unusual to see grandmothers on the bus get up and give their seats to teenage monks. In a paradoxical way, the renouncing of the world gives the monk an elevated status within it.

To understand this, we need to understand the essence of lay Buddhism in Theravada countries. Lay persons can, of course, always become monks.[3] But most choose to remain in the estate of life to which they were born. But this does not mean that they lack religious sentiments, nor that they do not participate in their tradition. Rather, they follow the path laid out for lay persons—the path of merit (*punya*). In essence, the

---

[3] The lack of Buddhist nuns in present-day Theravada countries reflects an historical accident rather than deliberate sexism. Indeed, women still play a very effective, if unofficial, religious role in these countries. Moreover, a movement is strengthening to reintroduce the ordination of nuns in the Theravada countries. Nuns still exist in Mahayana and Vajrayana Buddhism.

Sangha and the laity are two halves of a single entity. The monks need the lay people to supply them with food, clothing, and the other prerequisites of life. The laity, on the other hand, need the monks as moral exemplars and a means of generating merit. But what is the point of this merit?

Here again we come back to the question of *karma* and rebirth. If one knows that one is going to be reborn, and that one's favorable rebirth is dependent on good actions, it is only prudent to accumulate as great a stock of good actions as possible. Within Theravadin culture, this is seen as being accomplished through *dana*, or giving. This giving is seen as being most effective when its recipients are monks. What has evolved is a symbiotic religious relationship that benefits both sides. Moreover, merit has other uses as well.

While Theravadins do not believe that gods can lead them to ultimate freedom, they are still seen as having their uses. When one needs help with the crops, sickness, love, and so forth, it is useless to consult the Buddha and his monks, since these worldly problems are not their area of concern. The gods can help, but they need to be coerced. This is done through the transfer of merit. Since Buddhists do not see the gods as immortal, only very longlived, they believe that the gods will be reborn just as they will. This being the case, the gods need merit as well if they are to be reborn in a good condition. But the nature of being a god makes it impossible, for a variety of reasons, to generate such merit. Thus the gods are dependent on human beings in that they can acquire merit only if it is transferred to them by humans. This the Theravadin Buddhists are happy to do in return for worldly considerations.

The emphasis placed on meditation for monks means that they spend much of their time separate from ordinary practitioners. But this is not always the case. On the great Buddhist holidays, the two groups interact. In general, Buddhist festivals are structured around events from the life of the Buddha. Moreover, since they developed within the context of agricultural societies, they also tend to bear some relationship to the cycle of planting and harvest. Other festivals, such as the beginning of the New Year, vary from one society to another.

In Theravada countries, regular fortnightly days based on the appearance of the full and the new moons are set aside for religious observance. These days, called *poya* days, correspond loosely to the European or American Sunday. On these days, lay persons observe the Five Precepts of not lying, killing, stealing, practicing inappropriate sexual acts, or taking drugs or liquor. Lay people often spend the day in religious pursuits such as going to hear a sermon delivered by a monk and practicing a small amount of meditation. This is the general pattern followed on all religious holidays, which occur on the *poya* days of particular months. *Poya* days are not celebrated in non-Theravada Buddhist countries.

For the Theravada Buddhist, the most important celebration of the year is the full moon day of May, known as *Wesak*. The birth, Enlightenment, and death of the Buddha are all believed to have happened on this day (albeit in different years). Another important festival falls on the full moon day of June. This marks the beginning of the three month long Rain Retreat (sometimes called the Buddhist Lent). At this time, the monks withdraw from society in order to practice meditation more intensively. Lay persons also attempt to adhere more strictly to Buddhist principles during this period. This period ends with *Kathina*, where lay persons bring the monks new robes and other necessities of life.

Some festivals are practiced only in certain areas. For example, the festival of *Poson* celebrates the bringing of Buddhist teachings to Sri Lanka in the second century B.C.E. Likewise the observance of *Esala* takes place only in Sri Lanka. It is marked by a huge parade in Kandy, called the *Esala Perihara*, at which time the holy tooth relic of the Buddha is displayed. In other Theravada countries, other local festivals take place as well. While these festivals are serious events, they are also enjoyable occasions.

Zen: The Way of Emptiness

Zen Buddhism stands in sharp contrast to Theravada Buddhism, both geographically and ideologically. The original home of Zen was India, but it was not until it was carried to China, and then to Korea and Japan, that it reached its fullest potential. The course which Zen initially followed was different from that of most other schools of Buddhism. These schools tended to congregate in monasteries which came to acquire more and more property over the centuries. Thus the monks found themselves in a peculiar position. Individually they were as poor as the Buddha's original followers. Collectively, however, they were often rich beyond the dreams of avarice. Increasingly, they sank these funds into large buildings, elaborately adorned and richly furnished. While this impressed outsiders, there was a growing feeling among some of the monks that such frills were dangerous distractions from the essential business of gaining release from the cycle of life and death. These new intellectual currents were to affect the development and orientation of Zen.

Philosophically, the essence of Zen is that all beings are already enlightened. They simply do not know it yet. The goal of Zen, therefore, is to awaken people to their own spiritual nature. This is accomplished, not through book learning or intellectual activities, but through meditation. Zen meditation is designed to overcome the rational, dualistic mind and to lead the practitioner to the unifying ground of existence which we all share. This can be done in one of two ways. In the Soto school of Zen, the practitioner "just sits," since this school believes that the very act of concentrated meditation is in itself sufficient to lead to Enlightenment. For the Rinzai sect, the process is a bit more complex. This school uses short paradoxical questions known as *koans* as a means of shocking individuals out of their dualistic thinking. Some of these *koans*, such as "what is the sound of one hand clapping" or "does a dog have the Buddha nature," have become famous even outside the Buddhist tradition.

This meditative training, along with Zen's emphasis on simplicity, might lead one to think that Zen has done away with the more ritualistic side of Buddhism. Indeed, it was this assumption that first attracted many American and European converts just after World War II. But this is not in fact the case. Zen was influenced by the wishes of its patrons, the wealthy and powerful ruling classes of Japan. These classes, who often saw religion and government as two sides of the same coin, were often more interested in Zen monks' perceived ability to perform powerful protective rituals than in the philosophical and meditative practices that they advocated. While this type of activity found its fullest expression in other Buddhist schools such as Shingon, all of the Japanese Buddhist schools were to some extent tinged with this ritualistic emphasis.

Consequently, ritual had, and still has, an important place in Zen Buddhism. In the monasteries and temples there is usually a morning and an evening service presided over by either the abbot, in the case of a monastery, or the chief priest of the temple. Lay persons can attend these ceremonies, but except for the great Buddhist holidays, they tend to be for religious specialists only. Fruit, flowers, and incense are offered to the Buddha and the major *Bodhisattvas* such as Manjusri and Avalokitesvara at these ceremonies. Various texts are chanted, particularly the **Heart Sutra**, a brief scripture that encapsulates the philosophical teachings of Zen. At these services, the officiants often wear gorgeous embroidered silk robes that seem very far removed from the austere life preached by Zen. All of this comes as something of a shock to American and European practitioners who have learned their Zen from books and not from living teachers.

As in the Theravada Buddhist countries, the monks and the lay people come together to celebrate important religious dates. But Mahayana Buddhist religious holidays often vary from those of Theravada countries. In Japan, the largest Mahayana country, the Japanese Buddhists do not celebrate the birth, Enlightenment, and death of the Buddha on the same day as their Theravada cousins in Sri Lanka and Southeast Asia. The

Shingon monks meditating in front of an altar at Shojoshin-in Temple, Mount Koya, Japan. Shingon monks are renowned for their ability to perform potent protective rituals.

Buddha's birth (*Hana Matsuri*) is celebrated on 8 April, his enlightenment (*Nehan*) on 15 February, and his death (*Rohatsu*) on 8 December. *Rohatsu* marks a period of one week of intensive meditation. Of particular importance to Japanese Buddhists is the four day festival of *Obon* which starts on 13 July. This festival commemorates the release of the mother of one of the Buddha's disciples from one of the Buddhist hells. In Japan, it has become a festival of remembrance of one's deceased ancestors. Some festivals are strictly of importance to Zen practitioners. In October is celebrated the festival commemorating

Bodhidharma, the first teacher to bring Zen from India to China. Great Japanese Zen teachers are honored as well. Rinzai Zenji is remembered on 10 January, Daito Zenji on 22 November, Dogen Zenji on 28 August, and Keizan Zenji on 15 August. Pure Land practitioners honor their founder, Shinran, on 21 May.

Vajrayana: The Way of Ritual Mysticism

Sometime around 500 C.E., another set of religious developments was taking place in India. It was at this time that both Hinduism and Buddhism began to exhibit those traits that we now term Tantra. Tantra seems to have been an attempt to develop a new form of practice which was more dynamic than the static meditations of earlier Buddhism. In the process, a radical new form of Buddhism emerged. Vajrayana Buddhism starts from somewhat different premises than other forms of Buddhism. This difference is not so much one of philosophy as it is of methodology. Vajrayana Buddhism, far from dismissing the body as a means of achieving Enlightenment, embraces it.

Consequently, the Vajrayana Buddhist monk's training is somewhat different from that of the Theravadin or Zen monk. The essence of Theravada training is the perfection of meditation through monastic regulations and the knowledge of the Pali scriptures. The essence of Zen training is the perfection of meditation through self-discipline. The essence of Vajrayana training is perfection of meditation through ritual practice. But this emphasis on ritual performance comes relatively late in the monk's career. First, he is required to undergo a long period of scriptural study in order to prepare for his ritual studies. Tantric practices are seen as extremely effective in leading the practitioner to *Nirvana*, but they are extremely dangerous as well. To approach them without intense preparation is not wise and can lead to reincarnation in one of the numerous Buddhist hells. It is for this reason that lay people tend to avoid Tantric practice, leaving its use to religious specialists.

Tantra is not something that can be done on one's own. It can be learned only at the feet of a guru who has himself traveled the path that the practitioner wishes to follow, and who can guide him or her by experience. Indeed, the guru is seen as being of such great importance that he is often venerated as a deity in his own right. Many of these highly developed gurus are seen as being able to reincarnate over and over again at will. These are the *tulkus* discussed above. Under the guidance of an experienced guru, the novice enters the Tantric path.

This begins with the preliminary practices. These practices may vary from school to school, but they have certain common elements. The practitioner must make 100,000 prostrations. He or she will perform 100,000 repetitions of various ritual offerings and repetitions of formulas designed to purify and focus his or her mind. But it must be remembered that none of these practices are actually Tantric in themselves! These practices, which necessarily take years and beyond which many people never go, are designed to test the would-be Tantric practitioner and purify him or her for the work ahead. This being said, the practices are also thought to have value in themselves, and many people, particularly lay persons, perform these rites without any thought of progressing beyond them to the actual study of Tantra, which is generally seen as the preserve of the monks and nuns. Such practitioners see these practices as bearing fruit in some future existence.

Having completed these preliminary practices, the student is now ready to be initiated by his or her guru. This ritual, the *abhiseka*, is central to the student's study. Without it, even if one had access to the Tantric texts, one's study would be in vain. The *abhiseka* not only authorizes a person's practice, it empowers it as well. Perhaps more importantly, it places the student in the "family" of those who use the particular text or texts named in the ritual. This qualifies the practitioner to receive the oral teachings that have passed down from teacher to student concerning the meaning of the text. This is very important. In modern society, we believe that texts should be self-explanatory. But in the Tantric traditions, the text was seen as far too dangerous to be clearly explained in itself. The knowledge contained in the text could cause real damage. As a result, the texts were often written in confusing and enigmatic language sometimes called **twilight language**. This meant that the texts themselves were not the primary vehicle for transmitting the teaching, but rather served as a sort of memory aid for the teachers and students in the study of the much more important oral tradition.

It is at the time of the *abhiseka* as well that the student receives his or her *mantra* and the *mandala* of his *yidam*. Vajrayana Buddhists appear to believe in a vast pantheon of gods and goddesses. But for the practitioner of Tantra, these deities are not so much actual existing entities as what we would call archetypal symbols for psychological processes and neuroses. As such, they provide the practitioner with a way of interacting with factors in his or her own mind that might otherwise only exist at an unconscious level, and thus be inaccessible in other ways. At the time of initiation, the guru, who is experienced with such questions, selects a *yidam* for the student to work with. Likewise, he shows the student the appropriate *mantra* for that deity. This *mantra*, usually of Sanskrit origin, encapsulates the essence of the *yidam* in a short phrase which the student can meditate on at all times and in all places in daily life. Through it, the student maintains a constant spiritual connection with his or her inner self.

The *mandala* is used in more formal religious practice. It is a very complex drawing which in effect unites the universe, in all its complexities, with the student. Through the *mandala*, a sacred space is created which unites the two. The *mandala* becomes a sort of sacred road map that describes the journey of the student to the "palace" of the *yidam*. By ritually and meditatively following this map, and overcoming the various obstacles that confront him or her, the student moves closer to the ultimate goal of uniting with the *yidam*. Such union is the culmination of the student's practice. Through it, he or she comes to recognize his or her identity with Ultimate Reality and thus achieves release from the cycle of birth and death.

Rituals of this nature, such as the Kalachakra ritual, are not tied to the Buddhist year with its recurring religious holidays. The Tibetan calendar is lunar and so the days on which festivals occur can vary quite widely. The Tibetans celebrate the birth of the Buddha on the ninth day of the fourth month of the year. They celebrate his Enlightenment and death on the fifteenth day of the fourth month. On the fourth day of the first month, the Tibetans begin to celebrate *Monlam Chenmo,* which goes on for some three weeks. On the fifteenth day of the fifth month, offerings are made to local gods and goddesses who are believed to be the protectors of the Buddhist teachings. Of particular interest to the majority Gelugpa sect are the festival of the death of its founder Je Tsongkhapa on the twenty-fifth day of the tenth month and the birthday of the present Dalai Lama which is celebrated on 6 July of the Western calendar.

Pure Land: The Saving Grace of Amidabutsu

All of the paths that we have discussed up to this point are very difficult for the lay person to follow. They require that the practitioner leave society, and that he or she spend long hours in meditation or ritual practice in order to achieve the desired goal of Enlightenment. For the vast majority of people, this is neither an attractive nor a possible alternative to life in the world. Family and social obligations do not allow it. What hope, then, does Buddhism hold out for such people? Was supporting monks or engaging in preparatory practices the most to which they could aspire? Were they required, in effect, to postpone any hope of Enlightenment until a future incarnation? This question arose early in the history of Buddhism, and the answers that evolved were to give birth to perhaps the most widespread of the Buddhist schools—the Pure Land School.

The roots of the Pure Land lie in India. As we have seen in chapter 3, new ideas associated with the Mahayana school started to develop there sometime around 100 B.C.E. One of these new ideas was the concept that the universe that we inhabit was only one of many world systems. In the Buddhist scriptures, we read that near the end of his life the Buddha was strolling through the forest one day when he casually mentioned to his attendant Ananda that, if someone should ask him, a Buddha could live on in the world indefinitely. Unfortunately, Ananda was not the quickest of the Buddha's disciples and he failed to take the hint. Undaunted, the Buddha repeated himself. Again Ananda failed to make the appropriate request. The Buddha tried one more time and when Ananda still did not ask him to remain in the world, promptly informed him that he would soon die.

For Buddhists, the death of the Buddha marks the beginning of the decline of the power of the Buddha's message in our world. As time goes on and we become more remote in time from the period of the Buddha, the moral condition of the world continues to decline. Indeed, many Buddhists believe that it has declined so much that in the current age it is impossible to reach Enlightenment. However, not all world systems were like ours. The main reason for this was that each of these worlds had its own Buddha, and that the Buddhas who had incarnated in those worlds had not died as had the Buddha of our world.

This came to affect the whole goal of religious practice. For the Theravadins, the decline of this world meant that the most that they could aim for was a favorable rebirth in a future time when a new Buddha, Maitreya, will appear on earth to rejuvenate the Buddhist faith. But many Mahayana Buddhists had a more immediate possibility—rebirth in a different, purer universe. These universes came to be known collectively as the Pure Land. The Buddhas who had established Buddhism in these worlds had been gifted with disciples who were somewhat quicker on the uptake than poor Ananda. Consequently, these Buddhas continue to live forever. As a result, their worlds not only did not decay as our own had, but actually improved to the degree that, from our perspective, they were paradises. In fact, they were so perfect that anyone being born into such a world was inevitably able to progress spiritually to the point that they would achieve Enlightenment in the course of one lifetime.

The goal of Buddhists in this world, as the Pure Land Buddhists envisioned it, was to be reborn in one of these Pure Land worlds. However, there was a problem. Pure Land Buddhists believed that our world was so corrupt that nothing we could do on our own would be sufficient to ensure our rebirth in the Pure Land. Fortunately, human beings had supernatural allies in the Buddhas who ruled these lands, the **Dhyani Buddhas**. The most famous of these was Amitabha or, as he was called in Japan, **Amidabutsu**. Like all Buddhas and *Bodhisattvas*, Amitabha had taken a vow that he would save all intelligent beings. In his case, this meant he would aid anyone who called upon him with perfect faith to be reborn in his Pure Land. This would assure that person's achieving Enlightenment in their next birth.

At one stroke, this concept breathed new life into Buddhism. Meditation, ritual, and text study could be practiced only by those who could afford the large outlay of time that these methods demanded. This meant that they were open only to those who had either renounced the world or were independently wealthy. But the basic tenet of Pure Land, that salvation depended on faith more than works, meant that common people, tradesmen, and peasants could now enter fully into Buddhist practice.

There now arose a series of devotional exercises and literature aimed toward the class of people who had up to now been more or less relegated to the role of support staff to the monks and nuns. While the peasants could and did continue to gain merit through giving, they could also aspire to salvation through the aid of supernatural beings. Through the constant repetition of short formulas and prayers, the lower classes could both work and pray at the same time. This, coupled with pilgrimages to sacred sites whenever possible and the support of the monks became characteristic of the followers of the Pure Land path.

Pure Land never seems to have been a large school in India, but when it spread to East Asia its progress accelerated rapidly. Part of the reason for this was that both China and Japan produced many gifted preachers. Unfortunately, their championing of Pure Land doctrine was often seen as subversive by the ecclesiastical and lay authorities, who from time to time persecuted them. All of this only served to reinforce in the minds of the common people the idea that Pure Land Buddhism was the Buddhism of the people, whereas other forms of Buddhism were the Buddhism of the upper class. Consequently, Pure Land Buddhism spread extremely widely throughout the lower strata of society in China and Japan. It is not surprising, therefore, to find that Pure Land Buddhism was the first Buddhism to reach America as people from these classes emigrated in search of a better life.

Buddhism has had a long and interesting history but it would be unwise to assume that its glories are all in the past or that it is no longer a dynamic religion. As we shall see in this chapter, Buddhism has been forced to adapt itself to the swiftly changing conditions of the modern world. In some cases, the transition has gone smoothly. In others, however, the tensions between Buddhism and modern ideologies have not been resolved without severe difficulties.

Buddhism and National Identity in Sri Lanka

As noted above, Buddhism has a long history in Sri Lanka, and the religion swiftly became an established part of the culture of the Indo-European Sinhala people. Buddhism continued to solidify its hold on the Sinhala consciousness for several centuries. Indeed, it is in Sri Lanka that the scriptures of the Theravada school were first committed to writing in the first century B.C.E. It should be noted, however, that other schools of Buddhism flourished here as well. The Theravada school of Buddhism did not become the official religion of Sri Lanka until the time of Parakkama-Bahu I (reigned 1153–86 C.E.).

But it was during this time as well that the steady progress of Buddhism was interrupted by political upheaval. Sri Lanka began to experience the recurring invasion of the northern part of the island by Dravidian speaking Tamil peoples from South

India. These invaders were, by and large, Hindus who felt no compulsion to support the Buddhist religious establishment. As their influence waxed and waned through the centuries, so too did the fortunes of Buddhism in Sri Lanka. It is no surprise, therefore, that Buddhism came more and more to be associated with the Indo-European speaking Sinhala group, just as Hinduism came to be associated with the Dravidian speaking Tamils.

This association became explicit during the reign of King Dutugamuna (101–77 B.C.E.). It was during his reign that the Sinhala people regained control of much of the northern section of the island that had previously been wrested from them by a Tamil invader. In order to do so, Dutugamuna raised the standard of religious war, casting the conflict in terms of righteous Buddhist Sinhalas regaining their homeland from unrighteous Hindu Tamils. This was a pattern of rhetoric which was to be intensified and consolidated by subsequent kings until it became an article of faith within Sinhala culture. Thus a tension was created which was to bear such bitter fruit in Sri Lanka in our own time.

This pattern was further reinforced with the arrival of the European powers in the early 1600s. Driven by a mixture of commercial ambition and religious fervor, the European powers were to play an increasingly important role not only in Sri Lanka, but throughout all of Asia. The Portuguese were the first such colonial power in Sri Lanka. Conditioned by centuries of warfare against the Muslims in the Iberian peninsula during the period known as the Reconquista, they had come to associate their colonial expansion with the expansion of their own austere form of the Roman Catholic faith. Fiercely intolerant of all other religious expression, they carried on a vigorous program of eradication of Buddhist and Hindu religious sites, and of conversion (often forced) to Roman Catholicism. The Portuguese were soon displaced by the Dutch who promptly imposed their own Protestant religious preferences on the region. They in turn were followed by the British who were primarily interested in trade and felt that this interest was best served through the pursuit of a policy of religious toleration.

As colonial expansion increased, the political power of the Sinhala (and Tamil) peoples decreased until the only indigenous independent state was the kingdom of Kandy in the hilly center of the island. It was inevitable, given the religious prejudices exhibited by the invading European colonial powers, that the Kandyan kingdom was perceived as the guardian of Sri Lankan Buddhism. Moreover, Buddhism and political independence came to be intimately linked in the Sri Lankan mind just as it had in years past. This link became very important in the postcolonial period for the direction that Buddhism has taken in Sri Lanka.

The Modern Sri Lankan Experience

During the colonial period, Sri Lanka had seen its full share of Christian missionary activity. But the Buddhist *Sangha* had always been able to maintain much of its dominant position. Since most colonial activity was confined to the coastal regions of the island, the kingdom of Kandy, protected from intrusion by its surrounding palisade of mountains, remained a haven for traditional Sri Lankan life and culture and a lavish supporter of institutional Buddhism. All of this changed with the advent of the British. In 1815, with the memory of the threat of French and Dutch ships disrupting their lines of communication with their eastern colonies still fresh in their minds, the British proceeded to eliminate the Kandyan kingdom.

With the disappearance of this last official protector, the Buddhists found that they now served a new master who did not understand their ancient traditions. At first, this seemed to present no great problem. The British rulers of South Asia had no interest in the religious lives of their subjects. Motivated by the ledger rather than the Bible, they were satisfied if they received their duties and taxes. But events back in Great Britain were to change the colonial government's easygoing attitudes to religion.

One of the major causes of this shift of opinion was a wave of evangelical fervor which had swept through the country. Many influential people now believed that Britain had a moral responsibility to its colonial subjects. Given the tenor of the times, this meant that every effort should be made to bring the indigenous populations within the fold of Christianity. This left the British colonial government in Sri Lanka (and elsewhere) in a paradoxical position. On the one hand, they believed that the indigenous people would indeed be better off as Christians. On the other hand, they were bound by promises that they had given religious authorities in Sri Lanka at the time of the Kandyan conquest. Buddhism had become very much a state religion. Its growth in Sri Lanka was such that the king (or the government acting in his stead) held control of the monasteries' financial assets and served as the judge in interfactional disputes. When the Kandyan kingdom had been dissolved, these functions were taken over by the British who pledged to support the Buddhist religion as had its native predecessor.

But as the clamor for increased missionary activity in Sri Lanka increased, the colonial government found it harder and harder to fulfill this pledge. When the older generation of sympathetic administrators died or retired, their replacements felt less and less bound to honor this obligation. By 1840, missionary activity was in full swing. By 1860, with the tacit aid of the government, Buddhism was being forced more and more on the defensive. It is not surprising, therefore, that it is during this period that we see a change in Buddhist attitudes away from peaceful coexistence with the Christians, and toward a confrontational counterattack on the missionaries and their religion.

The initial impetus for this came from a rather peculiar source. Colonel Henry Olcott was an American Civil War hero who had become a follower of H. P. Blavatsky and one of the founders of a new religious movement called Theosophy that incorporated into itself many ideas taken from Hinduism and Buddhism. Convinced of the spiritual value of Eastern thought, he had sailed to India and Sri Lanka in 1880 to study it in its natural environment. Appalled by the inroads the Christian missionaries were making in Sri Lanka, he launched a successful campaign to organize Buddhist opposition to the new religion. This included the foundation of lay Buddhist organizations, Buddhist schools, and an organized refutation of the Christian

missionary position. In due time, he passed the torch to his pro-
tégé, David Hewavitarne, who is better known to history by his
religious name—Anagarika Dharmapala (1864–1933).

Dharmapala did more to revitalize Sri Lankan Buddhism
than any other single person in modern history. Nor did his
efforts stop at the coast of Sri Lanka. Deeply distressed by the
fact that the Buddhist holy places in northern India were in the
hands of Hindus, he organized the formation of the Maha Bodhi
Society to purchase and refurbish them. In the process, the sites
once again became centers of pilgrimage for Buddhists from all
over the world and this marked the beginning of the revival of
Buddhism in the land of its birth. In Sri Lanka, Dharmapala,
who never became a monk of the Buddhist Order despite living
like one all of his life, began to support the formation of lay
Buddhist groups for the practice of meditation. Since Buddhist
meditation had traditionally been the preserve of the monks,
this new trend toward lay involvement in religion brought
Buddhism more and more into the public arena.

As the agitation for political freedom escalated, it became
apparent to the politicians that Buddhism still greatly influenced the Sinhalese peasant population. A good example of
how far they were willing to go to exploit this can be seen in
the career of S. W. R. D. Bandaranaike. Bandaranaike had been
raised an Anglican, but he adopted the religion of his ancestors
as a useful adjunct to his rising civil service career.
Bandaranaike had even proposed before independence that the
proper language for studying Buddhism was not Pali or
Sinhalese (the language of the majority of the population), but
English! However, sometime between then and his election
as Prime Minister in 1956, he had become a born-again
Buddhist.

It was at this point that he and others like him came to present Buddhism as the normative religion of Sri Lanka. Needless
to say, this did not sit well with the more than 20 percent of the
island's people who were not Buddhists. The Christians, and to
a far greater degree the Hindu Tamil speakers of the north and
northeastern parts of the island, found themselves increasingly

politically isolated as politicians exploited sectarian differences. With this increased emphasis on religious differences, rioting broke out as the government began a deliberate shift toward isolationist policies. The legislation that began to be passed disenfranchised English in favor of Sinhalese, abolished the state mandated quotas that guaranteed the Tamils a significant share in educational institutions and the government, and started to promote Buddhism at the expense of other religions.

The results are still with us. Sri Lanka has suffered for more than a decade with a smoldering and bitter civil war which has often been waged through the appeal of both sides to religious principles. Nor does it appear that this will end any time soon. Not only does the government periodically mount military operations against Hindu strongholds in the northern and eastern parts of the island, but the Hindus retaliate with a campaign of terrorism in the Sinhalese-held parts of Sri Lanka. The tragedy of Sri Lanka is that Buddhism, one of the world's most pacific religions, has become a rallying point for violence and intolerance. Sadly, this is the case not only in Sri Lanka, but elsewhere in the Buddhist world as well.

Buddhism and Colonialism in Southeast Asia

We can see similar forces at work in Southeast Asia. The countries now known as Indonesia, the Philippines, Malaysia, Vietnam, Cambodia, Thailand, Laos, and Burma (Myanmar) had for many years been influenced by cultural currents emanating from India and, to a somewhat lesser extent, China. A number of historians in the earlier part of this century saw Buddhism (and Hinduism) as being carried into Southeast Asia on a wave of cultural imperialism. While it is true that the indigenous cultures of the region found these religions and other aspects of Indian and Chinese culture appealing, and so incorporated them into their own cultural traditions, it would be unwise to see this as an uncritical process or one resulting from outside pressure. These cultures appear to have absorbed these new religious forms on their own terms, and they seem to have modified these new traditions in such a manner as to have them become, to all intents and purposes, indigenous religions in their own right.

Buddhism presents a good example of this. Chinese records show that Buddhism was established on the coastline of Vietnam at a very early period, but the exact dates of its coming to the region are unknown. Yet it may very well be that it is from this region, as well as from Central Asia, that Buddhism first penetrated China. In any event, it is clear that Buddhism and Hinduism had traveled along the maritime trade routes to Southeast Asia at a very early date, probably starting in the second century B.C.E.[4] But it was Hinduism that first attracted royal patronage in the region, and it is for this reason that we have very little archeological evidence to trace the development of Buddhism here.

All of this changes around 1000 C.E.. After this date, Buddhism increasingly becomes the official religion of the growing nation states of Southeast Asia. In these areas, the more conservative Theravadin school based on the Sri Lankan model was the form of choice. By c. 1300 C.E., Burma, Thailand, Laos, and Cambodia had become Theravada Buddhist countries.[5] The practice of linking Buddhism with the state which had come to be a distinctive feature of Sri Lankan Buddhism was widespread here as well, partially as a result of local condi-

---

[4] Legend has it that Asoka sent two missionaries into Burma in the third century B.C.E. While there is no corroborating evidence in Burma to substantiate this claim, the nearness of Burma to the centers of Mauryan power makes such a claim very possible. If this is the case, then this likely marks the first penetration of Buddhism into Southeast Asia.

[5] Island Southeast Asia presents a different picture. Indonesia's indigenous religion which combined the worship of Shiva and the Buddha was beginning to come more and more under the sway of Islam. The Philippines seem to have been content to practice their various indigenous religions. Vietnam chose to follow a form of Mahayana Buddhism closely linked to China.

tions and partially due to the fact that Buddhist leaders in this area saw Sri Lanka as the senior center of their religion. In any case, Buddhism flourished and was nurtured by royal patronage.

All of this changed as the European powers extended their sway over the region. This was, however, a relatively late development. The earliest colonizers, the Portuguese and the Spanish who came to Southeast Asia in the late fifteenth century, did not at first attempt to totally dominate the region. They were satisfied with controlling the relatively small areas around their trading ports. Thus, despite the fact that they saw colonization and religious conversion as the same thing, they only affected small areas of the Philippines and Indonesia. More concerted were the nineteenth-century efforts of the Dutch in Indonesia, the French in Vietnam, Cambodia, and Laos, and the British in Burma, Malaysia, and Singapore.

Among the first to receive the unwelcome attention of the Europeans was Burma. In an escalating series of wars, the British progressively incorporated more and more of Burma into their Indian empire. By 1880, the old state of Burma had effectively ceased to exist. The French began their colonial efforts in Southeast Asia at about the same time. Supposedly in order to protect Roman Catholic missionaries in Vietnam, the French began a series of aggressive wars which gobbled up more and more Vietnamese territory. Although they tolerated the existence of a Vietnamese emperor up to 1954, by 1900 the French controlled not only Vietnam but Cambodia and Laos as well. Thus the only part of Buddhist Southeast Asia that remained independent was Thailand, and that only because neither the British to the west nor the French to the east would allow the other to possess it. As in Sri Lanka, Buddhism came to be intimately linked with the concept of nationhood in the popular mind, and would have a role to play in the region's fight to regain its independence.

Buddhism and the Retreat from the Modern World in Southeast Asia

The situation in mainland Southeast Asia displays a number of similarities with that of Sri Lanka. In Burma, Theravada Buddhism was the religious faith of the Burman ethnic group which made up some 75 percent of the total population of the country. It is not surprising, therefore, that the struggle to escape the colonial grasp of Great Britain was in some degree associated with the resurgence of Buddhism in the same way that it had been in Sri Lanka. In 1906, the Young Men's Buddhist Association was formed and this organization provided the leadership that was to lead the country to independence in 1948. But the Burma that was created at this time was by no means a monolithic Burman state. Some 25 percent of its population was of other ethnic stock, and many of these peoples had been heavily influenced by European missionaries and become Christian.

It is not difficult to understand why these constituent groups of the Burman state were hesitant to support any institution which would bolster Burman domination. Their fears were not decreased by the appointment of U Nu as prime minister of the new Burmese Federation. U Nu was a pious Buddhist to whom being Burmese and being Buddhist were identical. His vision of Burma's future was one associated with a sort of Buddhist Socialism. This led to an insurrection of the Karens, who were mostly Christian and wanted their own state. Early Karen victories in the early 1950s led to the appointment of Ne Win as the commander of the government forces. This was to be a momentous appointment.

Meanwhile, U Nu sponsored a Buddhist religious revival in hopes of promoting unity in the country. In 1956, Burma hosted an international conference of Buddhist luminaries to celebrate the 2500th birthday of the Buddha. This did not calm the anxiety of the minority groups who feared Burman domination, and increasingly, these groups, who tended to live in the mountainous marginal land that surrounded the fertile rice-producing river valleys, sought to gain autonomy from the central government. This, in turn, drove the government to place more and more power into the hands of the military. In 1958, the military under the command of General Ne Win took control of the country. An abortive attempt was made to return to civilian rule in 1960. It was at this time that the Burmese constitution was amended to make Buddhism the official religion of the country. But civilian government proved once again ineffectual, and in 1962, Ne Win took up the reins of power again, and they have remained in military hands to the present day.

At the same time, the military closed Burma off from interaction with the rest of the world. Except for brief periods of relative openness, Burma still remains one of the most isolated countries on earth. The resulting political climate has been one of unremitting oppression. All critics of the regime have been silenced either by intimidation or assassination. Nor have the Buddhist monks been exempt from such treatment. Consequently, the state-supported Buddhist Order has become little more than a government department. On the other hand, many dissident monks have joined resistance groups that oppose the government, and are very active in the struggle to return Burma to a democratic system of government.

The Buddhist relationship to the state was one of the key factors in the recent history of Vietnam as well, but in a somewhat different fashion. When the French had gained control of the area now known as Vietnam, Cambodia, and Laos in the late nineteenth century, they realized that they were going to need indigenous personnel in their administration. They turned to the relatively small number of Vietnamese who had converted to Christianity. When the region gained its independence, it was natural that the government be turned over to individuals with the experience to run it. Thus the Roman Catholic Vietnamese, who represented no more than 10 percent of the population, came to control the lives of the numerically much superior Buddhists.

In time the Buddhists, under the directions of activist monks, began to demonstrate for a restoration of Buddhist civil rights. The Catholic minority tried to hold on to power, but after a series of spectacular martyrdoms in which Buddhist monks calmly poured gasoline over their bodies and burned themselves to death, the Catholic government was deposed. Subsequent events, such as the Indochinese wars and the Communist takeover of Vietnam, curtailed but did not completely suppress Buddhism. Despite repression by the Communist government of Vietnam, the religion is still very much in evidence both in Vietnam and abroad among the immigrant communities of Europe and the United States.

Buddhism had been an honored part of Cambodian life for many centuries when that country resumed its independence in 1953. But in 1975, it suffered a blow from which it may never recover. In that year, the new masters of Cambodia, the Khmer Rouge, decided that in order to renovate Cambodian society they were going to have to eliminate all elements of society which did not lead directly to a socialist state. They proceeded to deport to the countryside and kill many of the country's educated elite. This included most of the Buddhist monks. In a brief reign of terror, some 15 centuries of Buddhist culture were almost completely eradicated. Only a few monks managed to flee the country in time. As a result, Cambodian Buddhist culture was kept alive in such diverse places as Long Beach, California, Lowell, Massachusetts, and Paris by a handful of monks. Today, attempts are being made to renovate Cambodian Buddhism in its homeland, but so much tradition has been lost and destroyed that it is questionable whether it will ever be restored to its former grandeur.

State Persecution of Buddhism in China

In China, the situation was somewhat different. Despite great initial successes, Buddhism was always suspect to the Confucian ruling class which continued to dominate Chinese government. Buddhism, as they saw it, undermined traditional Chinese family values, and donations to the various Chinese schools of

Buddhism reduced the tax base. It is not surprising, therefore, that Buddhism was periodically persecuted in China. As time went on, these persecutions took their toll. While among the peasants Buddhism continued to command a faithful following, it did so more on the strength of its supposed magical potency than because of a deep devotion to its metaphysical principles.

Consequently, when the Chinese reasserted themselves politically, they did so intellectually as well. New forms of Confucianism came to dominate Chinese thinking. Buddhism became more and more a rural religion practiced by the politically disenfranchised, and it never regained the intellectual stature which it had enjoyed in the seventh and eighth centuries C.E. But it would be unwise to conclude from this that Chinese Buddhist philosophical thought disappeared entirely. China's efforts to exclude foreign invaders and to reestablish its political unity drew a number of young monks into the struggle for modernity. Although they were never a majority of the *Sangha* and were often disapproved of by the official leaders of the Buddhist community, they were to have an effect on the modern development of Buddhism in China.

The most famous of these young monks was T'ai-hsu (1890–1947). He founded schools, promoted the study of Buddhist languages other than Chinese, and advocated the idea of a world federation of Buddhists. These efforts were beginning to bear fruit when China was taken over by the Communists. They saw the Buddhist monks and nuns as parasites who were draining the vitality of the Chinese people. In 1951, they confiscated most of the monastic lands and returned young monks and nuns to the lay state. In 1953, the Chinese Buddhist Association was formed to bring the Buddhist community under government control. Periodic campaigns of repression such as the Red Guard movement further weakened Buddhism in China. While Buddhism has lost much of its strength as a result of these persecutions, it still persists in China and will likely continue to do so in the forseeable future.

Buddhism in Modern Korea and Japan

Buddhism in Korea and Japan has been closely linked for many centuries. Indeed, it was often Buddhist monks from Korea who provided the link between Chinese and Japanese culture. By 1000 C.E., Son, a school of Zen Buddhism, had become the most popular form of Buddhism in Korea. Unfortunately, Buddhism was repressed by the rigidly Confucian Yi dynasty of kings (1392–1910). Strangely enough, it was the Japanese conquest of Korea in 1910 that marked the revival of Buddhist fortunes.

Although the Japanese allowed a resurgence of Buddhism in Korea, they attempted to force its development along Japanese models that were often quite different from indigenous Korean ones. This led to friction that eventually resulted in the formation of a unified Korean Buddhism in 1935. After World War II (1939–45) and the Korean War (1950–53), Buddhism was effectively eliminated in North Korea and to some extent curtailed in South Korea. However, Korean Buddhism continues to prosper despite these difficulties not only at home but also abroad.

Buddhism in Japan was to have its own share of difficulties in the modern period. During the period after the Meiji Restoration of 1868, Buddhism was ignored in favor of state-supported Shinto that glorified the Emperor. It was during this period that Buddhist clerical celibacy was made illegal with the result that today Japanese Buddhism is one of the few forms of Buddhism that allows a married clergy. It was during this period as well that Japanese Buddhism adopted many innovations from the West such as Sunday Schools, meditation clubs, young people's organizations, and, in some cases, the outward trappings of Protestant ritual and dress.

Another interesting development in modern Japanese Buddhism has been the rise of new lay Buddhist organizations such as Soka Gakkai and Rissho-koseikai. These new organizations have done away with the old organizational principles of Buddhism and replaced them with aggressive new methods that more traditional Buddhists find somewhat upsetting. On the whole, Japanese Buddhism has become a dynamic part of the national life. Moreover, a number of Japanese schools are finding fertile ground in Europe and America for their ideas and practices.

Buddhism and the Destruction of a Culture in Tibet

For many centuries, Tibet was viewed by China as a province of the Chinese empire. Satisfied with formal submission and the ritual exchange of gifts, China was content to allow the country to be governed by the great monastic orders as it had been for many centuries. All of this changed, however, when the Communists came to power in 1950. Dissatisfied with the traditional arrangements and anxious to secure its borders, the new Chinese government attempted to rule more directly. In order to do this, and consistent with their own atheistic ideology, they occupied the country, moved to suppress the monasteries, and disenfranchised the Buddhist religion.

In 1959, the Tibetan people rebelled. It was at this time that the present Dalai Lama fled Tibet and settled in India. The Chinese then embarked on a reign of terror designed to completely eradicate Tibetan Buddhism. Temples were looted, monasteries razed, monks tortured and killed, scriptures burnt. But extinguishing the Buddhist faith in Tibet proved to be more difficult than the Chinese Communists imagined. Monks began to make the long trek across the Himalayas into India carrying with them the invaluable texts of their faith. As they gathered in India, they reconstituted the ruined monastic colleges and began to teach a new generation of young novices the complex rites and rituals of Tibetan Buddhism.

Meanwhile, the Dalai Lama became an eloquent and charismatic spokesman for his country and his faith. By bringing his country's difficulties to world attention, he helped to popularize Tibetan Buddhism. Many Westerners, attracted by the rich and vibrant nature of the tradition, began to support Tibetan efforts to preserve their cultural heritage. While the politics of the Chinese

Many Westerners have been drawn to Tibetan Buddhism by its spiritual leader, the charismatic Dalai Lama, exiled in India since 1957. His high profile has helped to throw the spotlight on colonialist abuses by China in his homeland.

occupation of Tibet have yet to be resolved, it can safely be said that Tibetan Buddhism has managed to weather the storm. Through the courage and persistence of present-day practitioners, it will be preserved and passed on intact to future generations.

Planting New Flowers: Buddhism in Europe
and the United States

Buddhism is so much a part of modern culture, at least on a superficial level, that it is hard to imagine that as little as 200 years ago people in the West had almost no idea of the nature of this religion. It was not until the European powers began to carve out their colonial empires in South and Southeast Asia, and meddle in the affairs of the East Asian nations, that they began to pay attention to the indigenous belief systems of the conquered peoples. But generally this attention had little or nothing to do with the intrinsic worth of these systems. Rather, these early administrators saw religion as a means of social control. As time progressed, however, some Europeans came to appreciate Buddhism and the other Asian religions in their own right. As they began to master the classical languages of Asia, such as Sanskrit, Chinese, Japanese, and Pali, European scholars began to piece together what was to them a new and fascinating universe of thought.

This group of scholars tended to emerge from the lower ranks of the colonial administrators who spent most of their days dealing with the administrative problems of the common people over whom they ruled. Since there were very few other Europeans to socialize with, these officers often took up study of the local culture. A good example of this was the case of T. W. Rhys-Davids (1843–1922). An administrator in Sri Lanka, he spent his leisure hours learning Pali, the sacred language of Theravada Buddhism. What he found astonished him. The Buddhism that began to emerge from the texts was not the (seemingly) superstitious religion that surrounded him, but rather an elegant, subtle philosophy that resonated with the logical, scientific thought that was coming to dominate European thinking. He became so enthusiastic about his studies that he founded the Pali Text Society with the intention of editing the entire Pali canon and translating it into English. This is a goal that the Society (which still exists) has very nearly achieved.

The next major change in Buddhist–European relations came in 1879, when Sir Edwin Arnold published his famous epic poem, *The Light of Asia*. This was a retelling in English verse of the life of the Buddha, not from an academic standpoint but from that of someone who appreciated Buddhist teaching as religious expression. Soon after this, Helen P. Blavatsky, a Russian, and Henry Steele Olcott, an American, two founders of the religious movement known as Theosophy, traveled to India and Sri Lanka to study Eastern thought. In Sri Lanka, they participated in a ceremony that formally accepted them into the Buddhist faith. Although their understanding of Buddhism was somewhat peculiar, these new converts were enthusiastic.

But the Theosophists were on the tip of the iceberg, so to speak. From around 1850 onward, Europe and the United States began to enter a period of religious crisis. Increasingly, intellectuals (and those who fancied themselves intellectuals) were becoming dissatisfied with Christianity. Some took issue with the idea that the Bible gave a complete and accurate picture of the origins of humanity and the physical world. Others took issue with Christian claims to the exclusive possession of the means of salvation in this world and the next. Many others simply wanted to replace what they thought of as mere superstition with a more scientific worldview. For many, Buddhism's "sudden" appearance on the intellectual horizon offered an answer to their dilemma.

But these early enthusiasts in Europe and America tended to misunderstand Buddhism. As we have seen, Buddhism does not suggest that more powerful beings than humans do not exist. Rather, it simply asserts that their influence is limited and that *ultimate* salvation lies elsewhere. Early European and American adherents to Buddhism tended to interpret Buddhism as being completely atheistic and self-oriented. This was certainly not the case for many, if not most, Buddhists. It is not surprising, therefore, that early converts to Buddhism tended toward Theravada Buddhism where "supernatural" elements seem to be the least pronounced. When Europeans began to investigate Buddhism seriously in the middle of the last century, they were very attracted to the Pali scriptures of this school of Buddhism. This was because they saw modern European thinking embodied in these ancient works.

As we have seen, this is not precisely the way in which Theravada Buddhism has been played out in its indigenous setting. But this early European viewpoint has just enough truth in it to have made Theravada Buddhism an attractive option to many European and American seekers who could not accept an otherworldly component to their spiritual quest. The first of these converts to actually be ordained as a Buddhist monk was Allen Bennett (1872–1925) who was ordained in Burma. He was soon followed by a number of other Britons and Germans who embraced the monastic lifestyle. But it was not until after World War II that other forms of Buddhism began to make their way into European and American society.

The war itself was the major contributing factor to this new renaissance of European and American interest in Buddhism. The war brought Europeans and Americans into contact with other Buddhist countries such as China and Japan. Buddhism from these countries had already made a small beachhead in Hawaii and the West Coast of America. Unfortunately racism tended to keep these immigrant communities separated from the mainstream of American life. All of this changed after the war.

The first of the great Buddhist invasions of North America was the Zen craze that swept 1950s America. Zen had come to America with the attendance of the Japanese monk Soyen Shaku (1859–1919) at the great World Parliament of Religions held in Chicago in 1893. Meeting there with the enthusiastic publisher of religious materials, Paul Carus, this monk agreed to sent one of his disciples to help Carus with the translation of Japanese Zen Buddhist texts. This disciple was to spend much of his life introducing Zen to the West. His name was D. T. Suzuki (1870–1966).

Other Zen masters were to follow Suzuki to America in the period before World War II, and they soon gathered small groups of enthusiastic American disciples. But it was the Beatnik generation that emerged after the war which took Zen to its heart.

Writers from this movement, such as Jack Kerouac, Gary Snyder, and Allan Ginsberg, became ardent publicists for Zen (at least as they understood it). Alan Watts (1915–73), a wandering Jack of All Religions, also preached the gospel of Zen to an appreciative audience of youthful enthusiasts (mainly in California) during the late 1950s and 1960s.

This initial groundwork led to an influx of Zen teachers into America in the decades that followed, These teachers established Zen training facilities that taught Zen in the oldfashioned, rigorous Japanese manner. While something of a shock to an earlier generation of seekers who saw Zen as a "do your own thing" sort of religion, the Zen now in America has, as a result of this second wave of teachers, come more into line with traditional expressions of the religion. Indeed, a number of Americans have been recognized as Zen masters in their own right. It might even be said that there is a new type of Zen, American Zen, emerging under their guidance.

Nor should the contributions of the Chinese and Korean Zen schools be forgotten. In California, Zen Master Hsuan Hua (1908–) founded the Sino-American Buddhist Association and the Gold Mountain Dhyana Monastery where the training is very traditional and very rigorous. Other teachers, such as Sheng Yen Chang, are also spreading the teachings of Chinese Zen to America. Likewise, Korean masters such as Soen Sa Nim (1927–) are revealing the treasures of the lesser known Korean tradition. Soen Sa Nim established the increasingly popular Kwan Um school (named for Kuan-yin, the *Bodhisattva* of compassion) in 1972. He was preceded in 1967 by Samu Sunim with his Toronto-based Zen Lotus Society.

Just as World War II marked the beginning of the penetration of Zen into America, the Indochinese wars of the late 1960s and 70s mark the beginning of a new appreciation of Theravada Buddhism. During this period, American armed forces serving in Vietnam used the neighboring country of Thailand as a rest and recreation spot. Here they came in contact with Theravada Buddhism. Likewise, the increased American presence in Southeast Asia led to a growing number of Peace Corps volunteers being sent to the more stable countries in the region. All of this resulted in an heightened awareness of Theravada.

At this time as well, a number of people such as the American meditation teachers Jack Kornfield and Joel Goldstein went to these countries, and to Sri Lanka, to study and even to be ordained as Buddhist monks under such great contemporary Theravadin teachers as Ajahn Chah in Thailand and Taungpulu Sayadaw in Burma. Eventually, many of them returned to Europe and America, either to reenter lay life, or to teach as ordained monks. The Theravada Buddhism that they taught, however, was somewhat different in nature from that of the countries in which they had trained. There, lay persons did not, by and large, meditate—that was something which was done by monks. But in America and Europe, this was to become the primary religious activity of monks and lay persons alike.

On the other hand, many traditional lay activities associated with Theravada Buddhism in its home countries did not find a home among Europeans or Americans. The people most drawn to Theravada Buddhism were often persons who were not comfortable with traditional religion, particularly its institutional and supernatural aspects. Just as had been the case earlier in the century, it was the perception of Theravada Buddhism as an "atheistic" and "scientific" philosophy, rather than a religion in the traditional sense of the term, that was attractive to this new set of followers. As a consequence, many of the more devotional aspects of Theravada Buddhism were not adopted by these practitioners.

But for many people, the austere meditative practices of the Zen and Theravada varieties were unappealing. These people were looking for a more colorful Buddhism than these two traditions provided. For them, the answer to their search for religious meaning lay in Vajrayana Buddhism. This form of Buddhist expression was the least known of the Buddhist schools and the one which was the last to come to the West. Content to remain isolated in its Tibetan homeland, Vajrayana Buddhism might have remained unappreciated by outsiders had it not been for the national catastrophe which overtook it in 1950.

Right from the first, those Tibetan monks who had left Tibet for India were faced with a severe problem. The Chinese were systematically destroying their entire religious culture. Horrible stories emerged, most of which are unfortunately all too true. They told of monasteries burned, monks tortured and killed, and priceless works of art smashed. These activities became even more pronounced in the late 1960s during the Chinese Cultural Revolution. The Tibetan monks needed to find a way in which to preserve their cultural tradition. Replacing their depleted numbers was no real problem. Tibetans continued to enter the religious life, as many still do today. But how to support these monks now that the great Tibetan monasteries and their holdings were gone? What could be done to replace their texts, many of which were unique to the Tibetan tradition? The answer, the Tibetans swiftly discovered, lay in the West.

Thus in the 1960s Tibetan monks began to teach in the West. The most famous of these early missionaries was Chogyam Trungpa (1939–87), a *tulku* of the Kagyu order. He established the first Tibetan *gonpa* (monastery) outside of Asia, Samye Ling, in Dumfriesshire, Scotland in 1967. From this humble beginning, Trungpa created the far-flung Vajradhatu organization dedicated to propagating Kagyu Tibetan Buddhism in the West. After a serious car crash from which he never completely recovered, Trungpa married and left Britain for the United States. The more numerous Gelugpa school was somewhat slower in sending out feelers to Europe and the New World. The first teachers of this school to gain disciples in the West were Thubten Yeshe (1935–84) and his disciple Zopa Rimpoche (1946–) who founded the Foundation for the Preservation of the Mahayana Tradition in 1971 and Wisdom Publications, a well-respected publishing house now based in Boston.

But it was in the United States that Tibetan Buddhism really flourished. In 1951, a group of Kalmyks, fleeing from their former homes in postwar Russia, were allowed to settle in New Jersey. Since the Kalmyks had been for many centuries followers of Tibetan Buddhism, it was here that the first Tibetan Buddhist temple in America was established, presided over by the

Gelugpa monk Geshe Wangal (1901–83). This led to the first formal teaching of Tibetan and Tibetan Buddhism in America when, in 1967, Geshe Wangal's disciple, Geshe Sopa (1923–), was invited by the great Canadian Buddhologist Richard Robinson to join the faculty of the newly established Buddhist Studies Program at the University of Wisconsin. Geshe Sopa, in turn, arranged for the Dalai Lama to come to the United States in 1981, and in that year the Dalai Lama presided over a Kalachakra Initiation which some 12,000 people were said to have attended.

In 1970, Chogyam Trungpa, wearied by constant internal struggles in his European organization, migrated to the United States. At Boulder, Colorado, he established a new international Vajradhatu organization. He was succeeded as head of this organization by his American disciple Osel Tendzin (1945–90) whose profligate lifestyle and subsequent death from AIDS underscored the dangers in the unquestioning obedience to the guru taught by the Tibetan tradition. More orthodox in his approach was the Gelugpa master Kalu Rinpoche (1905–89) whose saintly personality and rigorous traditional approach to Tibetan Buddhist training began to produce the first group of authentically trained Western Vajrayana monks qualified to run their own training establishments.

It was in America as well that Nyingma Tibetan Buddhism found a new lease of life. In 1969, Tarthang Tulku established the Tibetan Nyingma Institute in Berkeley, California. He was soon followed by other notable teachers of the school, including its supreme head Dudjom Rinpoche (1904–87). One of Tarthang Tulku's major projects was to edit and publish the enormous corpus of Nyingma scriptures, a goal that is currently well on the way to completion. This, along with other similar ventures such as Wisdom Publications, has ensured that the immensely rich scriptural tradition of Tibetan Buddhism will be preserved for future generations.

Finally, a word must be said concerning the fortunes of Pure Land Buddhism. This school of Buddhism has been part of the American scene since the mid-nineteenth century when Chinese and Japanese workmen began to be brought to the United States to work on the railroad and in the cane fields of Hawaii. Over the years, it has acquired many trappings reminiscent of Protestant Christianity, not only in the West but even in the lands of its birth. By and large, it has remained in the Asian community. Most non-Asians who are attracted to Buddhism are drawn to the radical difference of its core message from that of Christianity and Judaism. Thus Pure Land Buddhism, with its many apparent similarities to these traditions, does not seem as appealing as more exotic forms of Buddhism. Nevertheless, its traditional followers are still numerous, particularly the Japanese school of Jodo Shin-shu, under the title of the Buddhist Churches of America (founded 1899).

Facing the Challenges of a Changing World

Buddhism is no different from other world religions in that it faces challenges in the modern world as well as opportunities. The twentieth century has not been kind to Buddhism. Large areas of the Buddhist world have disappeared due to political and social changes. A good example of this is China, where Buddhism had once been widespread. After the Communists took power, Buddhism (and all other religions) was systematically suppressed so that it is difficult today to discern how many Buddhists still remain in that huge country. As we have seen, the Communists carried their dislike of Buddhism to Tibet in 1951 where they attempted to stamp out Buddhism entirely, often by extraordinarily violent  means. Likewise during the hideous excesses of the Khmer Rouge in Cambodia between 1975 and 1979, virtually the entire Buddhist monastic Order was murdered along with perhaps as much as half of the entire population of this Theravadin Buddhist country. Many estimate that at the end of this period, out of an initial 80,000 monks, only a few hundred managed to survive. In China, Cambodia, and Tibet, temples were destroyed, scriptures burned, and valuable pieces of Buddhist art sold to the highest bidder.

Terrible as this overt attempt to destroy Buddhism has been, it is eclipsed by a more concerted and subtler assault on the

Cultural Synthesis in Western Buddhism

ONE OF THE NOTABLE FEATURES of the developing Buddhism in the West is the degree to which women teachers have taken a leading role in transmitting the teachings. While women have never been excluded from Buddhism, the male-oriented nature of most Asian societies has assigned them a subordinate role in religious matters. In the West, this is not the case. Indeed, many of the pioneers of Buddhist scholarship, such as Mrs. Caroline Rhys-Davids (1858–1942) and I. B. Horner (1896–1981), are still remembered as notable scholars. However, it is as religious teachers that Western women have come into their own.

One particularly interesting example of this was Jiyu Kennett Roshi (Peggy Teresa Nancy Kennett, 1924–96). British by birth, Kennett Roshi trained first in Western music at London's Trinity College of Music. Increasingly dissatisfied with the life of the Western world, she began to study Buddhism. One of the first women to receive the approval of Japanese and Korean Zen masters, she was authorized by them to teach. In 1969, she traveled to the United States and founded Shasta Abbey in northern California. Since then, her organization, the Order of Buddhist Contemplatives, has founded a number of other monasteries and temples. She wrote a number of books such as *Zen is Eternal Life*, *How to Grow a Lotus Blossom*, and *Diaries of Years in Japan*.

One might assume from this that Shasta Abbey would be a faithful recreation of a Japanese monastery, but this is not the case. Kennett Roshi decided early in her career that Buddhism needed to be adapted to the particular conditions of the West. For her, trained as she was in classical Western art and music,

A nun and monk caring for babies at Shasta Abbey, northern California. The monastery attempts to fuse Buddhist practice with classical Western traditions.

this meant taking Western forms and imbuing them with a Buddhist spirit. Hence one finds at Shasta Abbey that the monks and nuns wear robes that resemble those worn by Christian religious orders. Likewise, the music of the various services is based on Gregorian plainchant, not on Eastern musical models. One might rightly ask if this is the proper way to go about adapting Buddhism to the West, given the fact that these forms no longer resonate with the bulk of the population. Nevertheless, Kennett Roshi's attempts to place Buddhist spirituality within a traditional Western context shows the dynamic spirit of American Buddhism, and suggests paths for future development.

religion. This has come through the medium of Western culture. Smuggled in on the backs of Mickey Mouse and Michael Jackson, the Western gospel of consumerism is entirely at odds with Buddhist values which preach simplicity, tranquility, and turning away from the relentless acquisition of goods. But the Coca-Colonization of Asian societies has left them awash in rock videos, Western nightclubs, and expensive electronic consumer goods. While certainly not bad in themselves, these things sound a not-so-subtle counterpoint to the traditional Buddhist values of simplicity and disengagement with the world of the senses.

They do this by replacing Buddhist ideals with their own vision of the nature of human happiness as the pursuit of "stuff": the idea, as one sardonic philosopher has observed, that "the person who dies with the most toys wins." Along with these cultural values comes the worldview that supports them. This Western scientific worldview, with its discounting of religious values and its emphasis on the material here and now, has had a powerful effect on many of the Buddhist countries' educated classes. These groups have in many cases rejected Buddhism, equating it with the superstitions of the rural agriculturalists. This too has had an adverse effect on Buddhism.

Need we fear, therefore, that Buddhism, like so many religions before it, will disappear? The answer to this is that such an event is very unlikely. Over the centuries, Buddhism has shown itself to be highly adaptable to new cultural conditions. As we have seen, it spread from its original home in India throughout most of Asia, coping with new cultures and new languages as it encountered them. In the process, it became an integral part of these cultures. Even now, it is changing and adapting. The Buddhism that came to America and Europe from various Asian cultures is being reconceptualized and revitalized in such a manner as to make it uniquely a part of these cultures.

Likewise, Buddhism is adapting to the changing environment in its homelands as well. Whereas for many years it was seen as being outside the normal flow of secular society, Buddhist groups whose main concern centers on secular social problems are now springing up. A good example of this is currently taking place in Thailand. The Thais are in the process of transforming their economy from an agricultural one to a more industrial model. Unfortunately, as the European experience with the Industrial Revolution showed Westerners, this change is often accompanied by a fearful cost in the quality of human life. Thailand is finding this out. A particularly severe example of this is the ecological problems the country is now facing. Large tracts of land are being deforested as their trees feed the demand for wood products in Japan and elsewhere. This, in turn, is resulting in other problems such as erosion. In order to combat this, Buddhist groups headed by monks are addressing environmental concerns stemming from the country's rapid industrialization. Using nonviolent but innovative techniques such as ordaining trees (even Westernized Thais still hold the *Sangha* in respect and would not cut down an "ordained" tree), these groups are lobbying for saner use of natural resources based on the Buddhist respect for the integrity of all living beings.

In Sri Lanka, monastic organizations are becoming more involved in community health and other social issues in the many tiny villages which dot the island. Traditionally associating with lay persons only to teach and preach, many Buddhist monks are now concerning themselves with more mundane problems. Two good examples of this are Venerable Pandita Walgowwagoda Wimalabuddho Thero of Sri Wardhanaramaya monastery and Venerable Medagama Dhammananda Thero of Asgiri Mahavihara monastery in Kandy.

Pandita Wimalabuddho is a member of the highest council of the Buddhist church in Sri Lanka, but his interests extend beyond purely spiritual matters. One of the programs that he has been instrumental in supporting has been a joint program with Japanese Buddhist organizations to combat eye diseases in rural areas. These diseases, which if left untreated cause blindness, have always been a problem in the humid tropical climate of the island. Their treatment, which involves the simple application of antibiotic ointment, while relatively cheap is still beyond the means of the average poor farmer even if he or she understood the mechanics of the disease. Through the generosity of Japanese Buddhists, these antibiotics are being sent to Sri Lanka and are being distributed to the villages.

Nor is this the only example of Buddhist engagement with contemporary problems in Sri Lanka. Venerable Dhammananda represents a change which is sweeping through the Buddhist *Sangha*. A young, well educated man, Ven. Dhammananda was not content to remain in Sri Lanka but traveled to Taiwan to experience Buddhism in that setting. On returning to Sri Lanka, he began to work with lay people on a variety of social issues. He is emblematic of a change of attitude among younger Buddhist monks as a whole, namely that Buddhism demands engagement with the world, not retreat from it. Nor is this attitude restricted to religious specialists. In Sri Lanka the *Sarvodaya* Movement has been formed by Buddhist lay persons in order to address the socioeconomic problems found in the countryside. All of this heralds a new day in the relationship of Buddhism to its environment in this ancient society.

This reorientation of Buddhism is not happening in traditionally Buddhist countries alone. In the United States, Buddhist teachers and lay persons are a persuasive voice in many areas of social concern. A good example of this is Buddhist work with AIDS sufferers. When the AIDS epidemic first burst on the American scene, it appeared to be a disease almost exclusively associated with homosexual men. Since homosexual behavior was condemned by traditional Christianity and therefore poorly understood or appreciated by the bulk of the American public, AIDS patients were often isolated from traditional spiritual caregivers. Moreover, as the epidemic spread to intravenous drug users, this stereotypical association of "sin" and AIDS became even more widespread.

Among the first religious groups to go against this prevailing tendency were the American Buddhists. Since Buddhism, by and large, did not have the concept of sin and did not condemn homosexuality *per se*, AIDS was not seen as being disgraceful or a just punishment. Rather, it was regarded as just another example of the painful nature of existence, and those suffering from it as fellow beings in need of compassionate treatment. Thus, practicing Buddhists, both gay and straight, were in the forefront of caregiving to AIDS patients. Needless to say, such actions, along with other similar activities such as aiding the homeless, have greatly enhanced the religion's reputation in the United States and Europe.

The Timeless Message of the Buddha

What are the factors which contribute to this continuing appeal of Buddhism, and more particularly its growing appeal to Europeans and Americans? The simplest answer lies in the fact that the problems which Buddhism first addressed some 2500 years ago are still with us today more or less unchanged. People still question the nature of life and its ultimate meaning. People still wonder why the good suffer and the evil go unpunished. People still ponder the unstoppable forces of nature and their relationship to human existence. For many of these searchers, the Buddhist analysis of reality and its practical program for achieving transcendence from the pains of human life are very appealing. But other religions, such as Islam, Christianity, and Hinduism, offer answers to these questions as well. What is unique in Buddhism?

One of the features of Buddhism which is attractive to many people, especially people raised in the scientific milieu of Western society, is that Buddhism does away with the idea of the "supernatural," a split between this world and some unseen, totally other, reality. The universe, says the Buddhist, is a vast system of processes, not things.

For the Buddhist, one can no more change the inexorable laws of cause and effect than one can hope to repeal the law of gravity. Such a viewpoint is extremely attractive to the Western mind which has been nurtured on scientific principles. Whereas other religions depend on the unproven (and perhaps unprovable) concept of a supreme deity, Buddhism has no such needs. Moreover, Buddhist presuppositions seem to proceed much more easily from the generally accepted laws of physics, which increasingly seem to support many Buddhist contentions about the nature of the universe, than do theistic presuppositions. In many ways, Buddhist principles such as cause and effects seem merely to be physical laws applied to the metaphysical realm. Thus for many people Buddhism is an increasingly acceptable religious option because it is so "nonreligious," lacking many of the features that Westerners deem essential to religion such as that of a supreme deity.

Another reason that Buddhism maintains its popularity is that it tends toward individual rather than corporate expressions of religiosity. Among the Western religions, the core religious actions are defined as taking place in community. The believing Christian or Jew is enjoined to attend weekly services in association with his or her fellow believers. Buddhism, on the other hand, sees religious activity to consist of personal actions. The individual has, of course, opportunities to associate with and take comfort from the community of believers, but he or she can be just as good a Buddhist without ever encountering another coreligionist. It is the interior work of the individual that matters.

In the increasingly individualistic societies of Europe and America, this is a distinct advantage, particularly as demands on the individual's time increase and the stately seasonal cycles of ritual which mark Judaism and Christianity, geared as they are to the slow pace of agricultural societies, become increasingly impractical in a 24 hours a day, seven days a week industrial world.

Moreover the individual can practice as much or as little ritualism as he or she chooses. Whereas the bulk of Western religious activity takes place within the context of formal ritual, Buddhists can practice their religion without any recourse to ritual whatsoever if they choose (although very few people in a traditionally Buddhist country would choose to do so). On the other hand, those who do wish to support their meditation practice with more formal rituals can do so easily. There is a ritual style to suit all tastes in Buddhism, ranging from the relatively austere ritualism of Theravada to the ornate and complex ritualism of Tibetan Buddhism.

This appreciation of the personal in Buddhism plays out in other ways as well. Buddhism lacks much of the institutionalized prejudice that exists in other religions. Thus people of differing races, genders, sexual orientation, and lifestyles find a supportive atmosphere in Buddhism which they do not find in the Western religions. This is not to say that Buddhism is entirely free of the prejudices that assail other religions—such things as the present troubles in Sri Lanka are ample proof of that. Rather it is to say that there is no scriptural or institutional warrant for such prejudice, and indeed, much scriptural condemnation of such behavior. No Buddhist will be able to advance on the spiritual path through persecution of other religions, quite the contrary in fact.

Another appealing Buddhist trait is its long history of using everyday vernacular language rather than a sacred language understood by only a few specialists. This means that the scriptures of the religion are readily available to all of its members for study and reflection. This is not to say that the Buddhist scriptures are all of uniform quality or importance. But there is no privileged ritual language in Buddhism. The scriptures are seen as being just as authoritative in translation as they are in the original languages. In addition, the lack of a mediating priesthood means that each individual Buddhist possesses an equal potential for achieving realization of Ultimate Reality without needing to depend on another.

But perhaps the greatest strength of Buddhism is its commitment to peace. In a world that has had two major world wars and innumerable smaller conflicts in the last hundred years, the Buddhist call to peace and human reconciliation is particularly compelling. Buddhist leaders such as the Vietnamese monk Thich Nhat Hanh and the Dalai Lama are regularly nominated for the highest awards as a result of their activities on behalf of peace. Nor do these leaders preach a message of reconciliation between humans alone. They are also active in crusading on behalf of the mute inhabitants of our planet, demanding that we treat other species and the environment in general with the same respect that we wish for ourselves. In this, they offer a clear alternative to the prevailing human paradigm of exploitation, both of one another and of the earth.

There can be little doubt, therefore, that Buddhism will continue to remain a compelling advocate for a gentler world. As long as the problems that mark human existence persist, Buddhism will always find people in every generation for whom its message of hope, peace, and compassion still resonates. It will continue to offer such individuals a way of coping with life's many disappointments and tragedies, and an alternate model of human interaction with the world at large. For these people, Buddhism will always be the religion of many paths, but one goal—the goal of peace.

Glossary

Abhidharma   The third of the three divisions of the *Tripitika* or Buddhist canon. It deals mainly with philosophical problems.

abhiseka   (lit. "sprinkling") Ceremonies held mainly in Vajrayana Buddhism to initiate the student into a higher level of study. The number of initiations varies from one tradition to another.

ahimsa   The principle, first developed by Jainism, of nonviolence toward other living beings. Practices such as vegetarianism developed from this principle. Now a central tenet of Buddhism.

Amidabutsu   ("The Buddha of Endless Light") The central figure in Pure Land Buddhism. The ruler of the "pure land" where it is infinitely easier for Buddhists to achieve *Nirvana*.

anatman   The Buddhist belief that there is no immortal soul, but rather a "cloud" of sensations and processes which human beings mistake for a permanent soul.

anitya   The Buddhist belief that everything in the world as we experience it is impermanent.

arhant   In Theravada Buddhism, one who has reached *Nirvana*.

atman   The Hindu idea that there is an immortal human soul that is, in some sense, associated with *Brahman*.

Bodhisattva   In Mahayana Buddhism, a being who has completed all things necessary to enter *Nirvana*, but chooses to postpone his/her own reward in order to help other beings to achieve it as well.

Brahman   In Hinduism, the underlying motivating principle of the universe. Ultimate Reality.

Brahmanism   The first phase of Hinduism which was characterized by elaborate sacrificial rituals presided over by the brahmins.

brahmins   The highest caste in Hinduism. The priestly class.

caste   The Hindu idea that society should be divided into four hereditary classes.

Dalai Lama   The head of the Gelugpa school of Tibetan Buddhism. Nowadays, the acknowledged spiritual head of Tibetan Buddhism. The present Dalai Lama is the fourteenth of this lineage.

dana   In Theravada Buddhism, the most important lay virtue which consists of giving material goods liberally to the Buddhist monks.

Dhyana Buddha	The Buddhas of universes other than our own. Their name comes from the fact that they are mostly experienced while the disciple is in a meditative state. Important in the Pure Land tradition.
dorje	A small scepter, usually held in the right hand, which is used in many Tibetan Buddhist rituals.
duhkha	(suffering) The Buddhist concept that the world is characterized by more unsatisfactory experiences than pleasant ones.
Eightfold Path	The Buddha's practical answer, in eight categories, to the problem of the unsatisfactory nature of life.
Enlighten- ment	The goal of Buddhist practice. Other than the fact that Enlightenment moves one to a totally different reality, the Buddhists have relatively little to say about this concept.
Five Precepts	Buddhist ethics which apply to all Buddhists. They consist of refraining from killing, lying, stealing, improper sexual activity, and the taking of intoxicants.
Four Noble Truths	The basis of Buddhist thought: 1) life is unsatisfactory, 2) it is unsatisfactory because of desire, 3) there is a way out of the endless series of rebirths, 4) that way is the Eightfold Path.
ghanta	A small hand bell held in the left hand during many Tibetan Buddhist ceremonies.
guru	A teacher, particularly of religion. In Buddhism, a teacher is seen as being absolutely essential to spiritual development.
Heart Sutra	A central text of Zen Buddhism. The text of the Heart Sutra is so short that it can be, and is, chanted in its entirety at most Zen Buddhist ceremonies.
Jains	Early group of *Sramanas* whose organization and doctrines have many similarities with Buddhism.
Jatakas	The stories of the Buddha's previous lives before he became the Buddha. These tales often have a didactic message, but also serve an entertainment function in Buddhist societies.
karma	The idea that actions have effects which are inescapable, even if they do not bear fruit in the present lifetime. Karma is the Indian religions' answer to the problem of evil.
koan	A device, usually in the form of a question, used in Zen Buddhist training to force the practitioner to "turn off" the logical reasonable mind. Very often, there is no real answer to the questions that the *koan* presents.
Lotus Sutra	The central scripture of the T'ien-tai school. The Lotus Sutra was begun in India, but reached its most profound development in China.

lotus position The crosslegged position most approved for meditation practice.

Mahayana (lit. "the Great Vehicle) School of Buddhism which predominates in China, Korea, Vietnam, and Japan.

mandala A sacred drawing or design which provides the practitioner with a sort of "road map" of Reality. Much used in Tibetan Buddhist practices.

mantra A sacred formula used in some forms of Buddhist meditation. While common to all forms of Buddhism, it is particularly utilized in Tibetan practices.

mindfulness The foundation for all Buddhist spiritual practice. The idea that one must "wake up" and live life consciously and deliberately.

mudra Gestures made with the hands. Particularly important in Tibetan Buddhist ritual.

Nirvana The opposite of *samsara*, the world which we inhabit at present. The goal of Buddhist practice. Other than its being different in every way from anything experienced in this world, the Buddhists are hesitant to try to describe *Nirvana*.

Pali A dialect of Sanskrit. Pali is the language of the oldest collection of Buddhist scriptures and the sacred language of Theravada Buddhism.

phurba A ritual dagger used to cut off "ignorance" in Tibetan Buddhist rituals.

poya days The "Sundays" of Theravada Buddhism. They happen twice each lunar month on the day of the full and new moons. On these days, pious Buddhists perform a variety of religious actions including giving food to the monks, listening to sermons, and strictly adhering to the Five Precepts.

pratitya-samutpada The Buddhist concept that the world is not solid, but made up of an endless series of interlocking events.

puja In Hinduism and Buddhism, a ceremony designed to honor divine figures.

punya The idea that good actions produce merit. This merit, in Theravada Buddhism at least, can be "traded" to the gods in return for material favors.

Pure Land Sutras The collection of texts which describe the Pure Land. The scriptural foundation of the various Pure Land schools.

reincarnation The idea, common to all Indic religions, that human beings are "recycled" for lifetime after lifetime. Far from being a good thing, it is seen as something to be escaped from at all costs.

Rig Veda The oldest of the Hindu Scriptures.

Rinzai   One of the two predominant schools of Zen Buddhism. The Rinzai school makes extensive use of *koans* in its training.

samsara   The world as we experience it. Something to be escaped from as quickly as possible.

Sangha   Strictly speaking, all Buddhists. In practice, the term tends to refer only to ordained Buddhist monks and nuns.

Sanskrit   The sacred language of Hinduism and India in general. Distantly related to English, Spanish, and French.

samadhi   The lower of the two stages of Buddhist meditation. Consists primarily of quieting the mind.

skillful means   A term common to all forms of Buddhism but predominant in Mahayana Buddhism. The concept that an advanced Buddhist sage can use actions which appear wrong or immoral to lead disciples to the greater good of a religious life.

sky burial   The Tibetan Buddhist belief that leaving a dead person out to be devoured by birds is an act which will give the deceased good *karma* in their next life.

Soto   The second of the great schools of Zen. Unlike Rinzai, Soto Zen tends to eliminate use of the *koan* and concentrates on "just sitting."

Sramanas   A religious movement which broke away from the prevailing Brahmanic school of Hinduism. It is from the *Sramanas* that both Buddhism and Jainism developed.

stupa   A large mound of earth raised over relics of the Buddha. Popular places of pilgrimage.

sunyata   The Mahayana concept that ultimately nothing has any existence in itself.

Sutras   The second of the divisions of the *Tripitika*. The sermons and stories of the Buddha.

Tantra   A form of religious practice common to both Buddhism and Hinduism which places major emphasis on elaborate rituals performed by the individual practitioner.

Theravada   (lit. "the Way of the Elders") The oldest form of institutional Buddhism, Theravada places emphasis on meditation and a disciplined way of life. The predominant form of Buddhism in Sri Lanka, Burma (Myanmar), Thailand, Laos, and Cambodia.

Three Marks of Existence   The fundamental philosophical basis of Buddhism which says that 1) the material world is constantly changing, 2) human life is ultimately unsatisfying, 3) there is no permanent human soul that moves from one life to another.

Three Refuges The act of publicly declaring one's allegiance to the Buddha, his Teaching, and the Buddhist Order.

Tripitika The Buddhist canon. Refers to the three divisions of the canon into the *Vinaya*, the *Sutras*, and the *Abhidharma*, each of which was kept in a separate basket.

trsna The Buddhist idea that all unhappiness comes from desire (lit. "thirst") or greed for possessions.

tulku The reborn head of a monastic lineage in Tibet. The Dalai Lama is the *tulku* best known in the West.

twilight language In Vajrayana Buddhism, a deliberately obscure way of writing designed to protect its teachings from unauthorized practitioners. Twilight language can only be interpreted through the guidance of a guru or teacher.

Upanishads A series of philosophical writings first expounded near the end of the Vedic Period (c. 800–400 B.C.E.). A number of ideas found in the *Upanishads* are paralleled in Buddhist and Jain literature.

Vajrayana The third and latest of the major divisions of Buddhism, Vajrayana places a great deal of emphasis on ritualism. Once much more widespread than at present, Vajrayana is currently practiced mostly in Tibet.

Vinaya The first of the divisions of the *Tripitika*, the *Vinaya* deals with the rules governing monks and nuns in Buddhism.

Vipasyana The second and higher level of Buddhist meditation designed to lead the practitioner to Enlightenment.

yidam In Tibetan Buddhism, a personal deity who plays a central part in the practitioner's meditative and ritual life.

Yoga A series of practical exercises designed to allow the practitioner to penetrate the nature of reality. Used in both Hinduism and Buddhism.

Zen A school of Mahayana Buddhism which places its emphasis on meditative exercises rather than scriptural study. Found predominantly in China, Korea, and Japan, in recent years Zen has been very influential in America and Europe.

This guide gives an accepted pronunciation as simply as possible. Syllables are separated by a space and those that are stressed are printed in italics. Letters are pronounced in the usual manner for English unless they are clarified in the following list:

a   fl*a*t
ă   *a*bout (unaccented vowel)
ah   f*a*ther
ai   th*e*re
ay   s*a*y
ear n*ea*r
ee   s*ee*
i   p*i*ty
ō   n*o*
oo   f*oo*d

Abhidharma: ă bee *dahr* mă
abhiseka: ă bee *shay* kă
ahimsa: ah *him* să
Amidabutsu: ă *mee* dă boot soo
anatman: ăn *aht* măn
anitya: ăn *ee* tyah
arhant: *ahr* hant
atman: *aht* măn
Bodhisattva: bō dee *saht* vah
Brahman: *brah* măn

brahmins: *brah* minz
Dalai Lama: *dahl* ee *lahm* ah
dana: *dah* nă
Dhyana Buddha: dee *ahn* ă *boo* dă
dorje: *dōr* jay
duhkha: *doo* kă
ghanta: *gahn* tă
guru: *goo* roo
Jatakas: *jah* tă kăz
karma: *kahr* mă

koan: *gō* ahn
Mahayana: mah hah *yah* nah
mandala: *mahn* dǎ lǎ
mudra: *mood* rah
Nirvana: *near* vah nǎ
Pali: *pah* lee
phurba: *poor* ba
pratitya-samutpada: pra *teet*
    ya-sah mut *pah* da
puja: *poo* jah
punya: *poon* yǎ
Rig Veda: rig *vay* dǎ
Rinzai: rin zah *ee*
samsara: sahm *sah* rah
Sangha: *sahn* gǎ
Sanskrit: *san* skrit

samadhi: sǎ *mah* dee
Soto: sō tō
Sramanas: *srah* mǎ nǎz
stupa: *stoo* pǎ
sunyata: *soon* yǎ tah
Sutras: *soo* trahz
Tantra: *tan* trǎ
Theravada: tai rǎ *vah* dǎ
Tripitika: tri *peet* ik a
trsna: *trish* na
tulku: *tool* koo
Upanishads: oo *pah* ni shǎdz
Vajrayana: vahj rǎ *yah* nǎ
Vinaya: *vi* nǎ yǎ
vipasyana: vi *pah* sǎ nǎ
yidam: *yi* dahm

List of Festivals

SEASON/DATE	FESTIVAL

Theravada Festivals

fortnightly on appearance of full and new moon	*poya* days: lay persons observe the *Five Precepts* of not lying, killing, stealing, practicing inappropriate sexual acts, or taking drugs or liquor. Also listen to a sermon and practice small amount of meditation.
full moon day of May	*Wesak*: celebrates the birth, Enlightenment, and death of the Buddha which are all believed to have happened on the same day (albeit in different years).
full moon day of June	Marks beginning of three month long Rain Retreat (Buddhist Lent): monks withdraw from society in order to practice intensive meditation. Ends with *Kathina,* when lay persons bring monks new robes.
	Poson: celebrates the bringing of Buddhist teachings to Sri Lanka in second century B.C.E.
	Esala: takes place only in Sri Lanka and is marked by a huge parage in Kandy (*Esala Perihara).*

Mahayana Festivals

8 April	*Hana Matsuri*: celebration of birth of the Buddha.
15 February	*Nehan*: celebration of Buddha's Enlightenment.

8 December	*Rohatsu*: celebration of death of the Buddha. Marks one week of intensive meditation.
13 July	*Obon*: important four-day festival which commemorates the release of the mother of one of the Buddha's disciples from one of the Buddhist hells. In Japan it has become a festival of remembrance of one's deceased ancestors.

Zen Festivals

10 January	Rinzai Zenji (Japanese Zen teacher) remembered.
21 May	Shinran, founder of Pure Land Buddhism, honored.
15 August	Keizan Zenji remembered.
28 August	Dogen Zenji remembered.
October	Festival commemorating Bodhidharma, the first teacher to bring Zen to China.
22 November	Daito Zenji remembered.

Tibetan Festivals

(The Tibetan calendar is lunar so the days on which festivals occur can vary widely.)

fourth day of first month of the year	*Monlam Chenmo* begins.
ninth day of fourth month	Celebration of birth of the Buddha.
fifteenth day of fourth month	Celebration of Buddha's Enlightenment and death.
fifteenth day of fifth month	Offerings made to local gods and goddesses.
Twenty-fifth day of tenth month	Festival of death of Je Tsongkhapa, founder of Gelugpa sect.
6 July (Western calendar)	Birthday of present Dalai Lama.

Suggested Further Reading

General References

I. FISCHER-SCHREIBER, F.-K. EHRAND, and M. S. DIENER, *The Shambhala Dictionary of Buddhism and Zen*. Trans. by Michael H. Kohn (Boston: Shambhala, 1991)
An indispensable reference text.

RICHARD H. ROBINSON and WILLARD L. JOHNSON, *The Buddhist Religion*, 3rd ed. (Belmont, CA: Wadsworth Publishing Company, 1977)
The standard scholarly introduction to Buddhism.

SANGHARAKSHITA, *The Eternal Legacy: An Introduction to the Canonical Literature of Buddhism* (London: Tharpa Publications, 1985)
An excellent introduction to the extensive Buddhist collection of scriptures.

JOHN SNELLING, *The Buddhist Handbook: A Complete Guide to Buddhist Schools, Teaching, Practice, and History* (Rochester, VT: Inner Traditions, 1991)
Full of practical information on current Buddhist masters and organizations.

JOHN S. STRONG, *The Experience of Buddhism: Sources and Interpretations* (Belmont, CA: Wadsworth Publishing Company, 1995)
An excellent introduction to Buddhist thought based on primary texts.

Current Buddhist Practice

ROBERT E. BUSWELL Jr., *The Zen Monastic Experience* (Princeton: Princeton University Press, 1992)
A detailed examination of the life of a Zen monk by a scholar who lived it.

JACK KORNFIELD, *Living Buddhist Masters* (Boulder, CO: Prajna Press, 1983)
Discussion of a number of Theravada Buddhist teachers and their practices.

GLENN H. MULLIN, *The Practice of Kalachakra* (Ithaca, NY: Snow Lion Press, 1991)

2: The Roots of Buddhism

MICHAEL CARRITHERS, *The Buddha* (Oxford: Oxford University Press, 1983)

WALPOLA RAHULA, *What the Buddha Taught*, 2nd rev. and expanded ed.(New York: Grove Press, 1974)
Still one of the best introdctions to early Buddhist thought.

NINIAN SMART, *The Religions of Asia* (Englewood Cliffs, NJ: Prentice Hall, 1993)
An excellent introductory overview of the Asian religious milieu from which Buddhism emerged.

3: The Early Historical Development of Buddhism

KENNETH CH'EN, *Buddhism in China: A Historical Survey* (Princeton: Princeton University Press, 1964)
Still the best introduction to the subject.

AKIRA HIRAKAWA, *A History of Indian Buddhism: From Sakyamuni to Early Mahayana*. Trans. and edited by Paul Groner (Honolulu: University of Hawaii Press, 1990)
A clear discussion of the subject.

JOSEPH M. KITAGAWA, *Religion in Japanese History* (New York: Columbia University Press, 1990)

DAVID SNELLGROVE and HUGH RICHARDSON, *A Cultural History of Tibet*, rev. ed. (Boston and London: Shambhala, 1968)

PAUL WILLIAMS, *Mahayana Buddhism* (London and New York: Routledge, 1989)
A good examination of the doctrinal development of this school.

4: Modern Buddhism: Many Paths, One Goal

STEPHAN BATCHELOR, *The Jewel in the Lotus: A Guide to the Buddhist Traditions of Tibet* (Boston and London: Wisdom Publications, 1987)
A comprehensive overview.

ALFED BLOOM, *Shinran's Gospel of Pure Grace* (Tucson, AZ: University of Arizona Press, 1965) Still a valuable resource.

RICHARD H. GOMBRICH, *Buddhist Precept and Practice: Traditional Buddhism in the Rural Highlands of Ceylon* (Oxford: Oxford University Press, 1971)

A useful study of Theravada Buddhism as it is actually practiced.
TREVOR LEGGETT, *Zen and the Ways* (London: Routledge and Kegan Paul, 1978)

5: Buddhism and the Challenge of the Modern World

RICHARD H. GOMBRICH, *Theravada Buddhism* (London and New York: Routledge, 1988)
A study of the development of Theravada Buddhism in India and Sri Lanka.
SHIGEYOSHI MURAKAMI, *Japanese Religion in the Modern Century*. Trans. by H. Byron Earhart (Tokyo: University of Tokyo Press, 1980)
DONALD K. SWEARER, *The Buddhist World of Southeast Asia* (Albany: The State University of New York Press, 1995)
An examination of Buddhism in modern Southeast Asia.
CHRISTOPH VON FÜRER-HAIMENDORF, *The Renaissance of Tibetan Civilization* (Oracle, AZ: Synergetic Press, 1990)
A sympathetic study of the Tibetans' efforts to reconstruct their religion after the Chinese invasion.
HOLMES WELCH, *The Practice of Chinese Buddhism, 1900–1950* (Cambridge, MA: Harvard University Press, 1967)
Takes up where Ch'en leaves off.

6: Buddhism in the Twenty-First Century: Old Wine in New Bottles

CHRISTINE FELDMAN, *Women Awake* (London: Arkana, 1989)
Looks at the emerging role of women in Buddhism.
RICK FIELDS, *How the Swans Came to the Lake*, 2nd rev. and expanded ed. (Boston: Shambhala, 1986)
The definitive study on the spread of Buddhism in North America.
KEN JONES, *The Social Face of Buddhism: An Approach to Social and Political Activity* (Boston and London: Wisdom Publications, 1989)
DON MORRALE (ed.), *Buddhist America: Centers, Retreats, Practices* (Santa Fé, CA: John Muir Publications, 1988)
For those who want to pursue a more "hands on" study of Buddhism, this is the place to start.
THICH NHAT HANH, *Being Peace* (Berkeley, CA: Parallax Press, 1987)
Anything by this great contemporary Vietnamese Buddhist teacher is worth reading.

Index